LONG DISTANCE CASTING

A Complete Guide to Tackle and Technique

John Holden

THE CROWOOD PRESS

First published in 1982 by
The Crowood Press
Crowood House, Ramsbury
Marlborough, Wiltshire

Reprinted in 1985

British Library Cataloguing in Publication Data

Holden, John
    Long Distance Casting
    1. Fishing
    I. Title
    799.1'2   SH439

ISBN 0-946284-00-8

Printed and bound in Great Britain by
A Wheaton and Company Limited, Exeter

Contents

Introduction to Casting 5

Distance in Perspective 8

The Foundation of Good Casting 11

The Basic Techniques of Casting 16

Casting with the Pendulum Swing 24

Choosing a Rod for Pendulum Casting 30

Zoned-Action Rods for Pendulum Casting 35

Rod Materials and Blank Design 41

Rod Rings and Fittings 48

Multiplier Reels 55

Fixed Spool Reels 64

Shock Leaders and Reel Lines 74

Sinkers 80

Terminal Rigs and the Baitsafe Capsule 85

Back Casting 92

Index 96

Introduction to Casting

Casting is the basic skill of rod and line fishing. In fact most people can hide a lot of deficiencies in the way they fish, but no-one can mask an inability to cast properly.

Sometimes a short cast will drop your bait just where you want it, but more often than not you will wish to benefit from the choice of range (e.g. short, medium or long) available to the good caster. In other words good casters switch on the power when necessary; bad casters, on the other hand, struggle . . . and then look for excuses to explain why they went home fishless while other anglers managed to fill their larders with cod, bass, whiting or bluefish!

If you cannot cast as far as you want to, make an effort to learn. Your entire approach to fishing will change: you should enjoy yourself ten times more and should expect to hook at least three times as many fish during the year.

Although many practitioners of long distance casting fail to capitalise on the technique's real advantage, CHOICE OF FISHING RANGE, by continually fishing at maximum range, the un-tamed distance caster is still likely to catch many more fish than the man who cannot top 80 yards with his best effort. For reasons which are not fully understood, there seems to be a band of productive water offshore of most beaches. Putting a figure on it is difficult, but as a rule you will find some of the best fishing lies between 100 and 150 yards out. English cod and bass, American striped bass and red drum, Dutch flatfish all sometimes show a strong preference for the deeper and quieter water well out from the shoreline; tantalisingly close—especially when they are feeding on the surface—yet beyond average casting range for the mass of sportsfishermen. Only one thing is more frustrating than to thrash out your bait 40 yards short of feeding fish, and that is to have another angler stand next to you and cast right into the shoal. A dozen fish for him and none for you is the best catalyst in the world for rethinking your casting technique.

Pure distance however, does not always pay off. A 175 yard cast which impresses everyone around you is pointless if the fish are running through a gulley just 90 yards out. The experienced fisher-man is never locked into such a blinding ego-trip that he ignores or simply fails to recognise other factors. Casting skill must be linked to a know-ledge of water and of fishes and their habits. Seasons, tides and weather play a major role in fishing of all kinds, and to reap big rewards in terms of fish and personal satisfaction you must learn to think in the context of long range casting, which boils down to knowing when to cast as far as you can and when to toss the bait just a few yards.

'Long distance' is a vague concept. Exactly what is a long cast? 150 yards is a realistic target for the surf fisherman casting 4–6 ounces. Lighter tackle —a 2 or 3 ounce metal lure attached to 12 lb main line, say—travels nearly as far on less powerful equipment used with essentially the same casting style. Baits reduce distance in proportion to their bulk. A 200 yard cast with sinker alone is ripped down to 140 yards on addition of a chunk of fish bait to the hook.

Freshwater fishermen casting plugs and metal lures across rivers and lakes have yet another concept of distance, but tackle for casting less than 1 ounce is still capable of 100 yards in reasonable weather. 2 ounce tackle really flies out there: with appropriate rod, reel and 8–12 lb test line, you could drop a metal lure on a bass some 150 yards away. Progress to a full surf outfit and enjoy easy casting to fishing spots normally accessible only by boat.

If you prefer, develop your skills beyond fishing. Tournament casting with surf tackle is a great sport, and although parallels with practical fishing are sometimes hard to relate to these days, there remains an essential link between thrashing a sinker across a grass field and casting a bait into water. The skills developed on casting courts make their mark in everyday fishing and some of the best fishing rods and reels on the market have a tournament pedigree.

Tournament distances are phenomenal. The current British record for 5·25 ounces of lead, 0·35 mm diameter main line (that is around 15 lb test), 15 lb test shock leader and unrestricted rod and reel is 260 yards. In unofficial practice sessions leading casters exceed 275 yards. Less than ten years ago a 200 yard cast hit the national head-lines. Today the same distance will not qualify you to cast in the National Finals.

5

The Author, John Holden

Casting long distance on a shingle beach, Suffolk, England.

How far can you learn to cast? After years of teaching casting all over the world, I am confident enough to make some predictions. The normally co-ordinated man equipped with basic but efficient surf tackle balanced to 5 ounces of casting weight can develop a reliable, stress-free 150–175 yards without baits. In practical fishing terms, depending on baits and the weather, that equates to an easy 110–150 yards option. You do not have to cast so far, it might be a mistake to do so, but at least you have a choice. Ladies and juniors can expect 100 yards . . . and I have met some powerful, hairy chested female anglers who can add another 50 yards!

Teaching yourself to cast presupposes that you know enough about casting mechanics and methods to interpret various styles and thus form

a personal technique of your own. That is not always easy. If you have seen good casters in action, copy what they do until your own experience suggests changes for the better. Best of all, find a coach with a proven record of successful teaching and training. It is a fair bet that he can improve your casting more in one day than you might otherwise achieve on your own in several weeks. But whatever road you travel, be confident. There are thousands of anglers no more talented than you and no more athletic, who can cast a very long way and now catch many more fish than ever before. You can join them. All it takes is determination and commonsense. The idea of this book is to outline mechanics of casting so that you can work out a system for yourself, then polish it to produce those 150 yard casts you

always admired but could never quite manage.

Ernest Hemingway observed that there are many who want to be writers—enjoying the benefits, kudos and riches of the successful novelist—but who do not want actually to sit down and write. Writing is hard work, after all. In a minor way, casting is the same. For every dozen anglers who would like to stand on the beach or lakeside and push out cast after cast—long or short, trouble-free, deadly accurate—only one is prepared to get out there with a fishing rod and actually LEARN. Those who make the effort find that results appear within two months of practising, say, twice a week for an hour. Good tackle is important, yet costs little more than second rate equipment. Apart from the rod or blank, most keen anglers already own the right tackle anyway.

It costs no more in Pounds, Dollars or Yen to be a good caster than a non-starter in the distance race, but it will cost you time, effort and hard work. The rewards are immense; the investment lasts a lifetime.

In this book fishing tackle also comes under the microscope. Although I do not subscribe to the theory that tackle alone makes the caster, I do believe that tuning and selection count heavily in the quest for top results, at whatever stage you are, beginner or expert. The wrong blank, too much handle, no blocks in the multiplier controller or too little line on a spinning reel can create havoc.

Distance in Perspective

Excellent fishing distances and tournament record casts are poles apart. For some reason, though, anglers who are interested in better results automatically compare their distances to those of winning competitors. They never stop to consider the vast gulf between beach fishing and pure casting over a grassy court.

Good fishermen are content with 130 yards or so with ordinary beach tackle and baits. Only 130 yards? Well, not one caster in a thousand drops a decent sized cod or drumfish bait that far every cast, and without fear of a backlash. Most distance claims you hear of or read about, are nonsense. 175 yards . . . 190 . . . even the magic 200 yards from a beach? Don't you believe it.

Even the world's champion casters would not try to cast a bait that far unless conditions were absolutely perfect. Yet it is common to read articles which imply that the writer thinks nothing of casting at least 190 yards every time he fishes. I have discussed distance with leading surf fishermen all over the world – men who hit the rod so hard that air friction burns line and who regularly top 250 yards in practice. Which of them claims to cast ordinary bait 200 yards? None of them do. 175 yards, then? Maybe, but it depends on bait size, wind speed, and whether they are on peak form.

You must appreciate that tournament power cannot be switched on regardless of where you go casting. The tremendous speed of a 200 yard-plus cast demands a solid foundation. Just as a rocket needs a launching pad, a monster cast needs firm ground underfoot. You will not find that on sand and shingle where ground clearance of the tournament pendulum arc is limited: unless the beach is flat the sinker will rip out a furrow. Just the extra weight of terminal rig and bait destroy the fine balance you need for perfect co-ordination.

The power input of a 200 yard cast over grass is slightly different from that of a 'normal' fishing cast. There is no time to waste during a full-blooded competition throw. Full power goes into the rod as early as possible. If you drive into the swing as hard as you can, distances certainly will increase which is exactly right for a record cast. The same exaggerated technique in the surf, however, will merely explode the bait.

The consensus opinion on the 200 yard surf casts is this: if you use a tournament rod, competition casting style, big sinker, ultra-thin line and the smallest bait that qualifies for the name, you might just get there. The wind has to be blowing a gale from behind you; the beach must be level and solid underfoot. But even then, do not bet on it. 200 yards with baits soaks up the same power as 250 yards with sinker alone.

Just how far can anyone expect to cast from the beach or across a lake? There is no straight answer because, as any experienced angler appreciates, too much depends on conditions, bait size and tackle specification. 80–90 yards with a whole mackerel or mullet bait is about as much as anyone could reasonably expect whilst casting from the restrictions of a cliff ledge. If the beach is open and you can use compact baits and a powerful style, 160 yards is still exceptionally good going and the very best surf men would not expect more than 175 yards.

Sometimes it's necessary to cast to an exact spot on the seabed. Bass feed in the hot water outlet of Sizewell Power Station on the Suffolk coast. It's a 140 yard cast at high tide. Poor casters don't catch bass here.

Less experienced casters lose heart when they hear these figures tossed into the argument. 'If the best casters can't get more than 160 yards', they say, 'what chance do we have? Maybe our present 80 yards isn't so bad after all.'

There is a myth about distance casting. Half as much power on top of that required to reach 100 yards does not result in 150 yards. Doubling initial effort will not produce 200 yards. If it worked that way everyone would fish at 200 yards and tournament records might exceed one mile!

There is a purely scientific method to explain the relationship between casting and effort but I prefer the alternative explanaition which admittedly is a down to earth simplification with technical details reduced to a minimum. The figures are not related directly to pure physics but instead reflect the feeling of power flow I sense when I am casting a surf rod.

Suppose I cast a sinker alone, without baits and terminal rig to reduce distances. 100 yards absorbs 1 Unit of power. 2 Units of power on the next cast increase distance to 150 yards. 3 Units produce 175 yards. You see, the farther you cast the less yards are achieved for the boost in effort.

Progress is smooth enough up to 175 yards but after that you work hard for very little measurable improvement, for at 200 yards, which swallows six times as much effort as 100 yards, the law of diminishing returns bites deep. The extra paces which take you out to 210 yards devour another 3 Units—a 50 per cent premium for a distance increase which, were it applicable to fishing, would make little or no difference to catch rate anyway.

Even in simple terms, the explanation is complicated and concerns an array of factors which interplay every time you cast, but the underlying fact is that many pressures increase as square, cubic or quadratic functions. Double the speed of the sinker as it leaves the rod, and forces holding it back may increase by four, eight or sixteen times. In practical terms, then, your casting distance builds up to a point where it becomes difficlut to wring another yard from the tackle. A slight improvement demands a vast amount of work. I call that point the Distance Barrier.

Cutting line and reel drag to a minimum pushes the barrier back. Taking away line altogether dramatically increases range which is why a cracked-off weight flys so far. In contrast, every time you raise line diameter and consequently must use a larger reel, the Distance Barrier creeps towards you. Problems break into full gallop when you attach even one small baited hook.

Long-casting surf anglers know that casts of

Dick Broomer of Sea Angler Magazine's casting school puts a beach fisherman through the basic mechanics of long range casting. A coach is the short-cut to success.

more than 150 yards with baits impose tremendous demands on man and tackle. You must have a strong rod, free-running reel, split second timing and absolute mastery of casting technique. The outfit usually owes more to casting than to practical fishing; it is heavy and insensitive and out of keeping with bite detection, fishing handling and general precision. Surf fishing is more an assault course than a day's enjoyment and, there is always the spectre of backlash and burned thumbs unless every cast is perfect; and there is also the additional problem that your baits will not stay on the hook.

Set your distance sights just 20 yards lower and return to a better effort/result ratio. Use ordinary fishing tackle which makes for better bite detection—it is more fun when you hook a fish, and exerts less physical strain on you during a prolonged spell on the beach. For these benefits alone it is worth considering 130 yards as a practical target for surf work, or indeed for long range lake and dam fishing as well. Do not bite off more than you can chew. Master the basics, achieve your first 130, then weigh up the pros and cons of learning to cast even farther. The majority of fishermen do not consider the effort worth their while. Having learned to cast a long way—and make no mistake, 130 yards with baits is an impressive performance—they turn their full attention to catching more fish.

I use separate tackle for normal fishing and

ultra-long casting. The fishing outfit has a built-in performance ceiling. I see no reason to destroy my fishing for the sake of a few more yards which are almost surely denied to me in all but exceptional conditions. I go fishing to catch fish rather than to cast as far as possible and I believe that most surf men share the same philosophy. Only on rare occasions will I step up to the most powerful casting tackle in my collection.

Tournament casting is interesting and immensely useful is assessing tackle and casting methods, but that is about as far as it goes. Casting a plain sinker over grass is rewarding, and can be a great ego-trip as well, but I suggest you leave your casting fantasies and over-powered tournament tackle at home when you want to catch fish. It is more enjoyable that way, and in reality your baits will not fall far behind those of your neighbour who is busting a gut to outdo everyone else.

Once you realise that there is a distance trap which affects all casters no matter how good they are, long-range casting assumes the right perspective. To refer back to the point about 80 yards being pretty good, we can see now that it really is unacceptably low. Anyone of normal physique who practices a sound style must boost his distances quite appreciably before running up against the Distance Barrier. Only beyond 130 yards in general fishing conditions will the struggle begin. If you are having to work hard now to top 100 yards, it could be because your technique and tackle are wrong; but more often than not it will be because of your technique alone.

Distances on the beach are hard to assess. What looks like 120 yards may be just 80 yards. Do not fool yourself about your true ability. There is a bitter taste in finding out that your casting needs improvement, but you have to be realistic. Go out to a field or a stretch of dry sandy beach and measure half a dozen of your normal casts. Pace them out—a BIG step is a yard. Now pace out 150 yards from the casting point. There is the target to aim for when you cast without baits to hold back the sinker. Looks a long way, doesn't it? Whoever reckoned that 150 yards is a mediocre performance obviously does not live down here with the rest of us mortals. Truly, in real life 150 yards is a very long way to throw a fishing line and those 250 yard-plus tournament casts do not detract from it one inch. The good news is that YOU can send out cast after cast at least 150 yards on ordinary fishing tackle.

On the other hand, pressures on our sport from pollution and commercial fishing force us to extend horizons. Good distances today may be too short to catch fish in ten years time. With that in mind, dedicated shore fishermen have started work on advanced tackle and techniques which add many yards to everyday beach distances. The 200 mark is still safe from exploitation but a handful of pioneering casters are looking towards 175 yards as a practical range in surf. Their methods—the full tournament pendulum casts especially—and tackle developed for both fishing and competition casting are so intriguing that I have referred to them in several sections of the book. Bear in mind, though, that you must learn to walk before you run; either that or you will need the kind of Band Aid that heals shattered confidence and empty bank accounts.

The Foundations of Good Casting

SELF CONFIDENCE

Right now, you may not be able to cast more than 80 yards. The idea of casting farther interests you; or perhaps your local fishing has changed considerably, forcing you and other anglers to change tactics. You can see that better casters are now picking up fish while you cast all day for little or nothing.

Perhaps you have already tried to cast farther, but without success. It looks so easy when the experts do it. You invested in the finest tackle, but those long casts still elude you. Nothing seems to work; long hours of practice are nothing less than sheer frustration, nothing more than miles of backlashed line and burned thumb.

Or maybe you have improved from 80 yards to a steady 120 yards over grass. Catches are better as well, but something is still missing. If only you could find an extra 30 yards from somewhere. Perhaps you would like to switch to the pendulum style too? Why, even the kids do it these days! The trouble is, you cannot seem to control the swing or the sinker hits the beach every cast.

Self-doubt, misconception and sometimes sheer jealousy prevent potentially good casters from escaping the lower ranks of surf men. They love the idea of casting a long way. Money is no problem: they will happily pay whatever it takes. Time? Well, nobody has too much of that, but keen anglers are willing to find the two or three hours a week it takes to learn a more efficient style. Five out of ten never achieve their target—which for most fishermen is round 150 yards—because when it comes to the crunch they do not really believe in themselves. Even men who are halfway there may give up because they too do not believe they are cut out for really big distances.

YOU can cast 150 yards at least. But you must believe you can do it. It is no good pussyfooting around. Take this casting challenge by the throat and find out just how far you can go. I am not going to kid you into thinking that you (or anyone

else picked at random from a million other anglers) are likely to end up World Champion. But I can tell you for certain that unless you suffer some catastrophic physical disability or are numbered among the tiny minority who are just plain dumb and unco-ordinated, you can put out 150 yard casts just as easily as any good caster does.

Physically, it is no harder than riding a bike around the block. If you can figure out how to drive a car, you have more than enough brain and muscular co-ordination to toss a sinker with a surf outfit. What you lack right now is the self confidence to go out and do it.

Confidence is a mixture of believing in your own ability, and knowing what to do. Most fishermen do not know how to cast. They have never thought about it. Casting is just something one does. They copy someone else, learn from Dad, or just pick up a rod and do what comes naturally. Inevitably when they try to cast farther—by doing the same thing harder, or with a different rod and reel—nothing happens and they either forget the whole thing or dream up a neat excuse: 'Those top surf fishermen obviously have some secret formula; they're natural athletes; they're just lucky.' Or maybe 'The rod companies give them special tackle.'

Forget all that. Clear your mind forever about exotic equipment, super strength, years of practice, good luck and talent. None of them has much bearing on long-distance surfcasting. Of course, the naturally adept, physically fit caster will beat you in developing a 150 yard cast. He will probably go on to 200 yards if he works. But because he gets there first, it does not mean you cannot catch up. He may not even know why he does so well—many excellent casters really do not understand much about technique in general or their own in particular.

Natural ability being the sole difference between good and bad casters is an exact parallel to

11

Two months of occasional field practice adds many yards to the cast. This fisherman raised his distances from 50 yards to 175 yards in just ten weeks.

the theory that enough monkeys bashing typewriters at random would eventually reproduce the works of Shakespeare. It is a neat concept, but does not make sense logically or statistically. Both ideas were dreamed up by frustrated casters or writers who could not come to terms with their own shortcomings.

If you are an 80 yards man, who wants to cast farther, has tried, but cannot manage, I will tell you why you fail. YOU DO NOT KNOW WHAT TO DO. That is all there is to it. It is nothing to

worry about, it does not mean you are stupid, nor will it stop you learning, but it is a statement of fact, since if you DID know what to do, and were then able to put the knowledge into practice, you would be throwing 120 yards at least. It is actually more difficult to keep distances down than to build them up. (I bet you do not believe that one, but you will before long!)

I will bet something else too: you opened this book in the hope of suddenly discovering the secret of casting—just a few words with power to transform you into a super-caster. All right, here they are: THE SECRET OF CASTING IS TO MAKE THE ROD DO THE WORK. That is the single irreplaceable feature of all good casts. Learn to make the rod operate efficiently, and you cannot fail to produce acceptable distances whatever your individual style turns out to be. Where do you find the necessary confidence? You do not. It will find you at the moment you first feel the rod working between your hands.

MAKING A ROD WORK

A fishing rod cannot 'work' in the accepted sense. Without your help it just lies there, inert, unbending, incapable of casting a sinker one inch. When we say that a rod works, we really mean that the muscular speed and strength we put in during the cast is efficiently channelled to the blank and onward to the sinker.

Whatever the strict dictionary definition of work may be, a good rod, cast properly, feels entirely different to one cast by the traditional overhead thump, which is the basic style of millions of untrained anglers. There is no easy way to describe the difference in feel between a 'working' rod and one cast traditionally, but an analogy may help:—

Loop a 3 inch diameter rubber band over your thumb. Draw your hands slowly apart. The band begins by stretching easily, then stiffens up, and finally loses all elasticity. Continue pulling and you will break it. There are three fairly distinct stages then: preliminary extension requiring little effort; mid-stage stretch accompanied by a definite and continually increasing resistance; and the final lock-up where, either you stop pulling or, the rubber snaps. Looking at it subjectively, you will find that the band feels sloppy, springy and then solid. The way in which a fishing rod responds to casting power is almost an exact copy of the band's reaction to thumb pressure.

The rubber strip obviously is not 'working' at all in the first stage of stretching. You can move your thumbs apart as quickly as you like, but the tension between them does not increase because a rubber band in its early stages of extension is incapable of transferring pressure. It does not matter how much force you use either, for as long as the band remains sloppy and rubbery it must act as a shock absorber.

Now, move on to the mid-stage. Here you can feel more tension between your thumbs. Moving your hands rapidly to and fro in this area produces a sensation that the band is 'working', or in other words, acting as a strong spring that resists thumb pressure. Notice that your thumbs seem to be pulling against themselves as well.

However, if you pull the band wide apart, slackness and even elasticity disappear and you can feel the band actually lock solid. It might just as well be a piece of rope. All you can feel is a direct pull. Pull harder and either the band snaps or you get tired. You cannot pull at maximum power unless the band is 'locked' at the end of its elastic limit. Power and speed applied beforehand are merely wasted—the band just absorbs them and elongates.

YOU CANNOT CAST A ROD THAT IS NOT LOCKED. Like a rubber band, every blank starts out with a sloppy shock-absorber action, stiffens up in the mid-compression zone, then locks. The old-style overhead cast applies power and speed too early, so that the blank merely sponges them up and prevents direct transfer of your power to the sinker. The pendulum cast and all other efficient styles extends the casting arc so that the blank is compressed close to lock-up point BEFORE main body power is applied. You feel the rod compress—just as you feel that band stretch—THEN you pour in the power . . . which flows directly to the sinker. On release, the powerful springiness of the blank adds a final flick of acceleration to the sinker and also smooths the flow of line from the reel, hence the lack of backlash on a free-running multiplier.

Now, why does good casting look so relaxed and easy? Simply because a small amount of body power applied to a locked-up blank produces far more sinker speed than ten times as much thrashed into an unlocked rod. The earlier in the cast you apply full power, and the shorter the arc you use, the more of the effort is sponged up by the shock-absorber stage. That is why overhead casters work so hard for so little. Why does the multiplier overrun? That absorbed power has to go somewhere. The rod jerks so badly that line surges off the spool—not too much problem if the sinker is whistling into the air at top speed, taking up the slack line. But it is not, so all those loose coils wrap around each other in a massive bird's nest.

If you blend these observations with the description of zoned action rods, you will see why the design evolved and how neatly it slots into the new casting techniques. Old-fashioned slow taper rods are sloppy, weak rubber bands that never do lock up. Pendulum zoned-action blanks move easily and positively through the three stages, lock up easily and do not have to be 'stretched' half a mile before anything starts to happen.

1 *Ready to go. Sinker hanging near blank, body coiled like a spring.*

2 *Pendulum outswing begins.*

5 *Body fully uncoiled. Weight has transferred to left leg. Rod has just passed the forward limit of the left hand, which is starting to pull down to the rib cage.*

6 *Maximum power generated by the arm punch-pull drives the sinker upward into its flight path.*

asting Sequence

3 *Inswing complete. Head turns immediately the sinker pause is felt.*

4 *Body starts to unwind. Rod is pulled forward and blank compression begins.*

7 *Line release point – the rod flicks straight.*

8 *Follow through.*

15

The basic techniques of Casting

BASIC CASTING EXERCISES

Pendulum casts are assembled around four stages of body and rod power. These are:

1. The pendulum swing which positions the sinker correctly relative to the rod and to the caster.
2. A sweeping turn of the body which compresses the rod almost to lock-up point.
3. A full-power javelin-like pull from shoulders and body which, using the leverage of the rigid butt and locked tip, accelerate the sinker powerfully into stage 4.
4. The final punch and pull of the the arms that flick the rod over and hurl the sinker high into the air.

The best way to learn them is in reverse, starting with the flick.

Arm action

Anglers use all kinds of bowling actions, body gyrations and wrist power to flick the rod over at the end of the cast. The only satisfactory technique is a co-ordinated punch and pull with full shoulder weight behind them. The right hand punches the butt upward and forward. The left hand pulls the butt cap down to the lower left side of the rib cage. Both hands act together, with equal power. Anglers who cling to the old notion that using the left hand spells disaster with a multiplier reel should review their ideas because if anything, the left hand action is the more important.

Let us put together a simple exercise for making the arms work correctly. At the same time you will also learn a little of how a rod should feel in mid-cast. We shall not reach full lock-up at this stage, but the system generates enough useful power to bypass initial blank flexibility. In zoned-action terms, you make Zone B work. Expect to cast about 90 yards with standard 5 ounce surf tackle, which is the right equipment for mastering all these exercises. (Use a zoned-action rod, well filled fixed spool or tuned multiplier loaded with 0·35–0·40 mm main line, and a strong shock leader)

Laying out the cast

Draw a line on the beach in the direction you aim to cast. Position your left toe six inches back from the line and your right toe on the mark. Angle your feet slightly towards the casting direction. Suspend the sinker on a 3–4 foot drop, and set the reel ready to cast. Toss the sinker on to the beach directly back from the marked line. Look at the photograph and check these points: that the rod tip is almost touching the beach; that the left hand is high with the elbow raised; that the right hand is straight; and that the leader between rod tip and sinker is taut. This is your starting point. Analyse it carefully because it is to be the foundation for a lot of important work.

1 *Refer to the layout diagram. Set out the tackle with the sinker and leader laid on the beach. Rod tip is low; left elbow is set high. The right arm is comfortably extended in line with the rod.*

16

2 *Turn your head and look into the sky. Pull the rod through, javelin throwing fashion, until the left hand reaches its forward and upward limit.*

3 *Punch and pull the butt so that the rod tip flicks over. Line release will be naturally timed.*

4 Hold the follow through position while the rod reacts to release. Maintain position until the sinker hits the water.

Settle comfortably into position and turn your head and look high in the air—about 40 degrees elevation—and slightly to the right of casting direction. Now, pull the rod forward ALONG ITS LENGTH, in JAVELIN STYLE, until your left hand is high and well forward, and the right arm doubles up ready to punch. Do not put in any real power. Do not try to lift the sinker off the ground. Just move positively and smoothly and keep your eye on the aerial aiming spot.

As your left arm reaches maximum elevation and extension along the javelin line, the right hand will automatically have bent and moved in closer to your chest. At the precise moment this happens, PUNCH upwards with the right arm, PULL downwards with the left. The right hand should finish at full extension, pushing up towards the aerial mark; the left hand will be close to the bottom of the rib cage. The result of this push-pull action is a firm, powerful but smooth flick over of rod tip, at which stage you release the line. You will find that release takes place automatically. Do not force it . . . just let it happen. The sinker flies off, and you do nothing until it hits the sea. Then stop the reel.

The important point is that the transition from javelin pull to arm action is not a one-two movement with a gap in between. The two should blend together with no perceptible hesitation, no sudden acceleration and no loss of confidence. Just practise this simple exercise until it feels right. Aim for good direction and height. Forget all about distance as that will come later. Feel the butt starting to work between your hands and sense the controlled springiness of the blank. You are actually using a much bigger rod arc than you probably suspect. Laying the weight on the beach overrides most weaknesses of the overhead style and its stunted rod action.

Adding extra body power and casting arc
Your arms have a relatively short operating zone, and they are nowhere near as strong as leg, back and shoulder muscles. You cannot generate a massive amount of speed and power on that final punch-pull flick even if you were to try, for it would be wasted due to blank's failure to lock. The road to longer casts lies in another direction: that of using your body, and extending the total arc of the cast. Do that by re-thinking the start of the previous casting exercise. Now let us add the power necessary to take the distances up to 130 yards or more, again, with no sense of physical strain, no backlashes, no self-doubt.

The diagram is a plan view of the cast's layout. We have been working on rod and sinker alignment 'A'. Now it is time to investigate the extra power available in the shaded area 'B'–'C'. Rod tip and sinker lay-out move clockwise from 'A', and as they progress into the new region you will notice that the sinker shifts around relatively farther than the rod tip, thus altering the leader angle. This is not strictly necessary but will help smooth the cast later on when you increase speed and acceleration.

There are two ways to position yourself and the sinker/rod tip. First—and most common—is to lay out the tackle, then set your feet. Learn to work the other way around: pick out your aerial target, align your feet, then SWIVEL AROUND at the waist and shoulders to drop the sinker to the beach. This may seem an academic point, but it is actually crucial to the whole cast.

By working from the sinker position, you do not feel anything happening to your waist, leg and back muscles. The cast tends to be too much overhead, bypasses the body muscles and reduces the arc. But if you set your feet and aiming mark, then deliberately swivel around from hips, knees and shoulders to drop the sinker on the beach, your body coils like a spring . . . and more important you can feel it doing so. Run a few tests each way and see how much more positive the second technique really is. Do not bite off too much arc to start with—lay the sinker somewhere in the middle of the shaded area.

Check the photograph. Note that the right and left arms are relaxed but straight, holding the rod butt comfortably away from the chest. All the body weight is on the right leg, which is bent at the knee. The whole upper body is coiled and ready to unwind; the rod tip is low. In all, the starting position is similar to the body rotation of discus throwing.

The cast itself is very easy; it is so easy that you might be tricked into over-analysing the movements. All you do is turn your head to face the aerial target (yes, it is going to make your neck stiff the first few times) and uncoil your body through into the javelin-like pull and arm action used in the preliminary exercise. Do not flick the rod too soon, or you will end up with a sideswipe which misses out on control and power. If you get your head right round, then uncoil your body like a spiral spring, the rod seems to follow you rather than move around at exactly the same time—you will sense it coming from somewhere behind your right shoulder. Pull it through, javelin-style and flick the butt over. That is all there is to it.

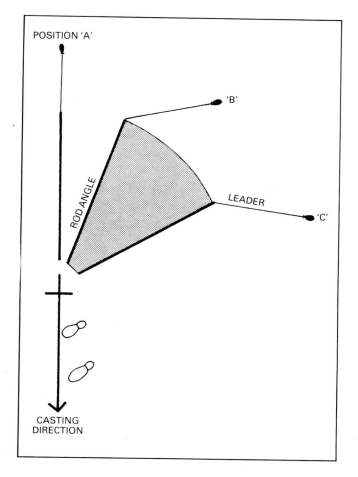

POSITION 'A'

'B'

ROD ANGLE

LEADER

'C'

CASTING DIRECTION

Spend plenty of time on this exercise, which is a good cast in its own right and quite capable of exceeding 175 yards. Experiment with various sinker drops and lay-out angles. See what happens when you reduce or increase the body rotation; feel the effect of transferring body weight from the right to the left leg as the cast progresses.

These two exercises are the foundation of good casting. After a couple of weeks practising the second technique with its extended power arc, you will be casting at least 110 yards easily and without backlash. Keep working, add power and speed, and you will top 130 yards. Then you can switch to the pendulum style, which in its simplest form is the same cast prefaced with a sinker swing rather than a ground lay-out. But most important—far more useful than pure distance right now—learn to control the cast. Aim for height, consistency and accuracy and at the same time get the feel of the rod working.

When you unwind your body, you will feel the blank start to bend smoothly. As the rod drives forward from behind your right shoulder and into the javelin-pull, the butt stiffens between your hands and the whole rod seems to tense up. That is the effect of body power flowing into the blank and locking down sections 'A' and 'B' of the zoned construction. A fraction of a second later, just as the arms take over, the whole rod seems to lock solid . . . and of course that means you punch and pull against the full rigidity of the butt section. It is a great sensation which guarantees excellent results. In fact if you do produce lock-up and solid leverage, the cast cannot go much under 130 yards, and the chances of a well tuned multiplier backlashing are minimal.

You have now learned to make a rod 'work' which is 90 per cent of good surfcasting technique.

Developing the off-ground cast

Extend the body rotation and rod arc until the sinker pulls around through 270 degrees or more, boost sinker speed with a long rod, and you have the South African style, the most powerful off-ground cast of them all, easily capable of hurling a 5 ounce sinker over 200 yards. If you fish clean, flat beaches where you can stand back from the water to cast, there is no overriding obligation to learn the pendulum cast. Just work through the original two exercises, and then build up to a full South African lay-out. When real power develops, switch to at least 12·5 feet of rod. This cast is slower than the pendulum but very powerful. In order to reap the benefit of the extra leverage, most South African experts prefer 13–13·5 foot surf rods.

1 Sinker and rod laid out. Left hand at shoulder level, right hand extended. The cast is ready to begin.

2 Turn your head and look upward toward the aerial aiming mark. Pull the rod forward javelin-throwing fashion. The left hand rises, the right begins to double up comfortably close to the chest.

3 Continue the direct javelin pull until the left hand drives to its foward limit. Notice that the rod hasn't swung around yet — the butt cap still points into the sky.

Action

4   The arm action begins. Left hand pulls down while *AT THE SAME TIME* the right hand punches upward.

5   The punch-pull continues, smoothly yet ever faster as the tip flicks over toward release point.

6   The punch-pull is complete. Line runs from the reel. You naturally follow through until the right hand is fully extended and the left stops close to the bottom left of the rib cage.

Body Rotation

1 *Refer to the layout diagram. The sinker and leader are at position 'B'. Note that the body is positively coiled—rather like a spiral spring.*

2 *The cast begins as usual with the head turning. This time, the forward and upward pull of the left hand and rod handle is accompanied by a powerful unwinding of the body.*

The Key to

3 *The longer rod and sinker arc, extra power from the body's uncoiling action, plus even more power drawn from the transfer of body weight from the right leg to the left to produce far more casting speed, which is felt as a positive 'tightening' in the butt as the left hand reaches its upward limit.*

4 *The cast ends as normal with a smooth, powerful punch and pull of the arms. Don't forget to hold the follow through position.*

Better Distances

Casting with the Pendulum Swing

Off-ground casts are of limited value in beach fishing and almost useless from lake and riverside. Undergrowth, weeds, boulders or swirling water prevent a neat lay-out and clean lift off. Yet good results depend on maintaining that long arc of movement that pre-loads the blanks. The pendulum swing overcomes all the drawbacks of the off-ground casts and also adds a little more speed and power. However, you should regard the pendulum swing primarily as the means of positioning the sinker, not as a power source.

The style is versatile and thoroughly practical, and overcomes the limitations of the cast already developed by the previous two exercises. You already have sufficient power and control to cast 150 yards at least. All the pendulum swing does is release that expertise for all-round fishing. The main power stroke and loading pattern of the new cast remains the same; all we do is to substitute a simple pendulum swing for the ground lay-out.

The new Sinker Position

Control of the pendulum is easier if you understand exactly what you are trying to achieve by swinging the sinker. The speed and momentum of the lead itself are secondary at this stage. Concentrate on sinker position and leader angle relative to the rod. Get them right, and the sinker itself automatically produces the inertia necessary to make the latter part of the cast flow smoothly and powerfully.

Set yourself up as if for the full off-ground cast with its extended casting arc. Lay out the sinker and leader as before. Make sure your body is fully coiled and ready to sweep the sinker into the air. Do not cast but imagine that instead of lying on the beach, the sinker is hovering in mid air, just out of sight, above and to the right of your head. Just visualise how it would sweep down to follow the sinker as you uncoil your body and pull the rod through to the final punch and pull. That is all there is to a pendulum cast . . . so let us make it happen. But first, note the exact position of the rod tip in the off-ground cast position. Do not guess at it but lay out a cast and then mark the spot with a handkerchief or coin. It is an essential reference point for the pendulum swing.

Re-adjusting the leader drop

Experiments during the preliminary exercises probably suggested a sinker drop of 5–7 feet between the tip and the sinker. This is about the right length of leader for most casters using an 11·5 foot surf rod, but it will not do for pendulum casting. Logically, you would conclude that the sinker must be swung on the shortest possible drop to avoid hitting the beach during the second half of the cast. Actually, the drop must be extended to permit adequate ground clearance. Most 11·5 foot pendulum rods work well with about 8 feet of free leader; and if in doubt, you are better off lengthening the drop rather than cutting back. Good casters always use very long drops on powerful rods, even with a standard length surf rod the working pendulum drop might be 9 or 10 feet. Some casters use a drop longer than the rod itself. To start, though, practise with 8 feet.

Producing a clean, smooth pendulum swing

Stand in your usual position on the casting line, coil your body around and down as if you were going to cast with the sinker on the beach, but this time hold the rod vertically in front of your face at a comfortable arm's length. The sinker, on the full 8 foot drop this time, will hang parallel to the blank. It may help later in the cast if you now adjust the rod position so that the reel is slightly above eye level.

If you have set yourself up exactly as before, except for rod grip and blank angle, the mark on the beach indicating the previous rod tip position will now appear slightly to the right of the vertical rod as you sight through. If it does not, swivel the whole upper body/rod unit right or left until it is correct. Do not move your arms and rod alone. Make a determined effort to rotate at the waist. Now you are ready to start the pendulum.

1 *The full extent of the outward swing should carry the sinker above eye level.*

2 *The inswing takes the sinker high behind the caster's head. The main cast begins when you feel the distinct pause in the pendulum action.*

PUSH the right hand firmly away from you, directly towards the mark on the beach. Move smoothly and quickly—but do not jerk—and you will generate enough force to lift the sinker well away from the rod on an outward pendulum swing which rises to at least eye level. As the sinker reaches the peak of its arc and hovers, PUSH DOWN WITH YOUR LEFT HAND AND LEAVE THE RIGHT ARM OUT-STRETCHED. Even a small downward press on the rod butt sweeps the sinker powerfully through a complete pendulum arc which takes the leader close to the right hand side of the rod, up past your right shoulder and out of sight. At the peak of its inswing, which you do not need to watch, you will feel a definite loss of tension on the rod tip. This pause indicates that the sinker has stopped climbing and hovers in exactly the right position for casting. It is your signal to GO on the rest of the cast.

It is worth practising the pendulum swing before adding the second half of the cast. Get used to setting up the rod and body, see how the right and left hands operate, feel for that definite pause in the inswing. Above all, make sure you work to a pattern. Too many anglers swing the sinker haphazardly to and fro, at any old angle, any height, in the hope that it will eventually hit the right spot and pause. That system never works. Aim for one clean outswing controlled by the right hand, a single inswing powered by the left hand pushing down: then you are ready to cast. Should something go wrong, drop the sinker to the ground by lowering the rod tip and then set up and start the whole rhythm again. Consistency is the key to pendulum smoothness and control. If necessary FORCE yourself to do it right. Lessons learned now are worth a fortune later in your casting career.

Putting it all together
This time, make your full pendulum swing, and as the sinker rises to the limit of its inswing and YOU FEEL THE PAUSE, turn your head, imagine the rod falling into the starting position used in the ground-cast exercise, AND CAST EXACTLY AS YOU DID THEN. Feel your body uncoil to load the rod then pull the butt forward, javelin throwing style, until your arms are in the correct position to flick the rod over. Do not rush because there is all the time in the world to get that sinker around and into the sky. The full cast is actually quite slow, especially at the start of the power flow which guides the sinker down from its pendulum position.

That is all there is to it. Does it sound like an anticlimax? Good because that is exactly what a pendulum swing should be. Thousands of casters look for problems which simply do not exist. By positioning that sinker where you want it, relying on the pause to trigger the next stage, and then falling into the now subconscious flow of the off-ground cast you practised to perfection, you eliminate the problems that inevitably plague casters who try to learn the whole technique in one piece. Think simple thoughts and just DO it. Of course you will need to practise. Take it easy, first get the feel of it, then turn up the power. Distance takes care of itself if you concentrate on smooth, relaxed flow. As in the earlier casting exercises, learn to feel how the rod reacts and loads during the entire casting arc. Also, remember that it is a waste of time to put in the final surge of acceleration until you feel the rod has locked up.

PENDULUM CASTING WITH LIGHT TACKLE

Casting under 2 ounce sinkers, especially on light rods, follows the same principles as those necessary to hurl big surf weights. There is one small change in technique: you do not need so much lower body power because the sinker just does not require that much arc or speed to produce good results. Most adults can simply reach a little farther back into the cast by straightening their arms, then bring the rod through the javelin pull and final flick on arm muscles' power alone, or with the addition of a positive weight transfer from right to left foot, which itself adds a significant boost to any cast. Run a few tests to see just how much body rotation and uncoiling action can be incorporated into your light tackle style. Under 1 ounce is virtually all arm power, but do not forget to extend the arc, especially if you use a baitcaster reel. 2 ounces is about the limit for pure arm action; 3 ounces is usually a full-power surf casting swing but you may not need quite as much sinker drop as for the 4 ounce-plus weights.

THE FULL TOURNAMENT PENDULUM STYLE

In principle the tournament style is an extension of the normal pendulum cast used for surfcasting. More power is derived from an extended body rotation and exaggerated pendulum swing. Top competitors use the same full 270 degree body rotation favoured by the South Africans. The sinker drop on an 11·5 foot surf blank would be at least 9·5 feet, and probably almost as long as the entire rod. Power build-up is rapid, so that the rod fully locks as early as possible, leaving room for terrific acceleration and leverage throughout the remaining arc.

1 *Begin by raising the rod slowly to vertical. The sinker hangs close to the blank. Make sure you know the outswing direction— see text for details.*

2 *PUSH the right hand away. A firm push outward will carry the sinker into its full upward arc.*

3 *Drive the sinker into the next phase of the pendulum arc with a firm PUSH with the left hand. Ideally, the right arm should remain straight, but you'll find it normally drifts backward a little. DO NOT deliberately PULL with the right hand—that would almost certainly result in loss of casting arc and reduced pendulum control. The sinker now climbs to its inswing limit.*

Inevitably, theory does not reflect the practice, time and effort necessary to hit those 230 yard-plus distances, and no two casters of that standard cast exactly the same way. The pendulum cast, tournament style, is therefore an ideal which the individual caster interprets as best he can. Learning the technique is a slow, steady process of trial and error using the simple fishing pendulum cast as the launching pad for personal development. I do not believe anyone can tell you exactly how to excel with these advanced techniques because to start with, this level of skill is self generating. Almost by definition, the winning casts result from new ideas and greater physical and mental conditioning. A coach can certainly pick out obvious flaws and bring out the best in a caster, but when it comes to the crunch, everything depends on the man who holds the rod. The greatest asset a tournament caster can have is an open mind.

THE MAJOR FAULTS IN CASTING

Negative feedback is the biggest block in casting. Too many anglers overanalyse their tackle and casting style. Instead of making it simple—and casting really is simple—they make life unnecessarily difficult by looking for faults that do not exist. I believe that if you understand the object of the exercise, which is to make the rod work properly, you can soon develop your own casting style. An individual's style is always a variation on a theme, never a carbon copy. Provided the theme is sound, the results have to be pretty good. However, there are a few faults which arise all the time, often with anglers whose techniques are basically healthy. For whatever value they may be to you, here they are, but please do not *imagine* you have them . . . get someone to watch you cast. We are all our own worst—and most innacurate—critics.

Most poor results are directly attributable to your failing to make the rod work properly. 90 per cent of the casters I meet with, or coach, suffer from this elementary mistake. Unless it is corrected, they never do cast properly. The main reasons are (roughly in order of likelihood):

1. *Too much power applied too soon through too short an arc.* Basically, this means you are using an overhead cast that relies almost exclusively on arm action.

2. *Not waiting for the rod to lock before applying full power.* Even if the off-ground lay-out of pendulum swings are correct, you lose out by snatching at the cast too early. Start slowly, build up smoothly until you feel the rod lock, then hit it.

3. *Directing the cast along rather than upwards.* This is a subtle one. When you cast easily, without trying for sheer distance, the cast flies high and straight. Add extra speed to the cast, and you start hitting low left casts, which may overrun or burn your thumb. The main reason is misalignment of the power line with the necessary angle of elevation, and that is caused by a progressively lazier left arm. If the left elbow drops, the cast flies low left. Correct it by making a positive effort to turn your head early in the cast and LOOK UP toward the aerial aiming mark. Drive the full power of the cast up into the air. That is how you gain those extra yards.

4. *Cutting the corner on the pendulum* is a serious fault. Rather than fall back toward the original off-ground cast rod position immediately after the pendulum swing, some casters hold the rod too high, then cut the corner of the cast, so that it finishes as a directly overhead thrash, almost like a vertical slice with a double-handed broadsword. The results include low left casts and burned thumbs (so you will need to decide between this fault and Number 3), snapped leaders and, in extreme cases, literally twisting the rod blank apart. The solution is obvious: regain the full casting arc.

5. *Misaligned pendulum swings* ruin any chances of a good cast. The most common error is to swing the sinker through an arc that lies at right angles to the rod, rather than almost parallel. This is a nasty problem, and frequently the destruction of an otherwise perfect cast. It is particularly prevalent in casters who use more body rotation than they can handle. In the same category come overshort leader drops they are a real menace. If you lose the cast or hit the ground, lengthen the drop and slow down.

Power Flow

1 *The sinker is poised at the top of the pendulum inswing. When you feel the pause, turn your head and look at the aerial target. You should have the impression of leaving the rod behind you—somewhere behind your right shoulder.*

2 *Pull the rod through JAVELIN STYLE, as before, and allow the tip to drop towards the mark on the ground (refer to text). Don't force it down; let it go there naturally . . .*

3 *. . . and you'll find yourself back in virtually the same position used in the off-ground cast. Continue the normal pull forward until the left hand is fully forward.*

4 *Then punch and pull as before. Compare this sequence with that of the off-ground cast. Pick out the common factors, and you'll see that the pendulum is only a substitute for the initial beach layout of sinker and leader. The power flow is almost identical.*

Choosing a rod For Pendulum Casting

Rods are everyone's favourite talking point. Hundreds of rods, blanks and fittings on the market offer surf and freshwater fishermen a bewildering choice. Yet the majority of rods are unsuitable for high-performance casting. Even in Britain, where the angling world is well versed in pendulum techniques and custom rod building, the average tackle shop stocks surf rods which are physically incapable of casting a long way. Most of them would snap or feel rubbery if hit hard with a pendulum-style swing.

The continuous stream of beginners and inexperienced anglers ensures that second-rate tackle eventually finds a home, usually with a man who had no initial idea of his poor investment. It is said that, in the British tackle trade especially, you can sell just about anything. Hundreds of uncaring, unknowledgeable dealers outsmart the angling public time after time.

Unless you know precisely what to look for in a distance casting rod or do-it-yourself kit, the odds are that you will end up with a pile of junk. However, this need not be the case, since good tackle costs no more than inferior tackle, and often is cheaper.

Specialist tackle shops all over the world offer excellent advice whether you aim to buy a ready-made rod or a set of parts. Leading dealers almost certainly offer a custom-building service—rods usually designed and finished to a standard far in excess of anything found in mass production. On the other hand, there are sharks in these waters as well.

Recommendation—product, manufacturuer and dealer—cannot be beaten. It pays in both time and money to search for a good supplier who understands your personal requirements. Some argue that it takes a good caster to know good tackle and it is no coincidence that the best shops are owned or staffed by anglers who spend as much time on the beach as behind the counter. Every tackle shop, wholesaler and manufacuer I have ever met who makes and stocks the best surf and general casting equipment has at least one man on the staff who speaks the right language.

The converse is also true: big, impersonal companies who produce and market second-rate equipment usually have nobody who really understands your problems. You get an answer all right, but it is obviously not born of experience or even of interest: 'Take it or leave it.'

Angling clubs, casting tournaments and fishing matches are an excellent source of basic information. If you want to know more about tackle, go there and ask. You will be surprised just how helpful other anglers can be. Most are quite happy to lend you their tackle for a few casts. Look out for manufacturer's demonstrations, magazine teach-ins (like the ambitious and highly acclaimed scheme run by Sea Angler magazine) and club lectures given by leading casters and fishermen. There is plenty of assistance available if you go and find it. Do not be afraid to write to columnists in the angling press or to consultants and field staff retained by the best manufacturers, but do remember to enclose a stamped addressed envelope for their reply.

Suppose you want to buy a new rod or kit right now. You do not know anyone who can lend you their tackle to try; local tackle shops are well stocked but not too helpful because chiefly there is nobody who really understands the difference between old and new-style casting tackle. A handful of simple tests applied to any blank or completed rod will eliminate trash and leave behind equipment which though perhaps not perfect, is at least capable of producing the right results. You do not risk spending good money on a soft, weak blank that is incapable of withstanding the power of a hard pendulum cast.

How to select a suitable blank for surfcasting
The tackle shop is filled with dozens of rods, both long and short, powerful and whippy, brightly finished and in kit form. All of them are labelled 'Surfcaster'. 'Take your pick', the dealer says. 'Carbon fibre rods are on the end of the line. Don't miss this week's special offer on Daiwa. I'll be in the back if you want me, but don't ask me about surf rods. Freshwater fishing's my scene.'

Custom-builders offer a fine range of casting rods for long-distance surfcasting. You can specify a blank action which exactly matches your physique and style.

Despite knowing little about surf rods, you can take some shortcuts. First, put all the carbon fibre rods to one side. Discard all those with carbon fibre tip sections. Glassfibre is a better choice for learning to cast and fish in the surf. Carbon (graphite) is actually superior in nearly every respect, but it is less tolerant of varying sinker weight and line test, and makes more demands on the angler, who must specify exactly which length, action and power of blank suits him and the way he fishes. Later on you may switch to a carbon rod. To begin with, ordinary 'E' glassfibre or, better still 'S' glassfibre, are just fine. They are versatile, virtually unbreakable, forgiving of error, and much cheaper than carbon fibre. The only exception is where the rod is made up of glassfibre tip and a carbonfibre butt. This is an excellent combination for any surf angler, experienced or beginner. The extra cost of a carbon butt is fully justified in terms of performance, weight saving and overall sensitivity. Fenwick Surf Sticks—in blank and rod version—are all made this way, and there is an optional carbonfibre butt now available for Conoflex and Carroll Zziplex blanks.

The majority of glassfibre blanks have either glassfibre or tubular aluminium butts, both adequate for surfcasting. Glassfibre will not corrode and usually imparts a little more 'feel' to the cast. Aluminium is the cheapest way to make a butt rigid and thus offers top-level casting performance (almost as high as a carbon fibre butt) at low cost. Drawbacks are lack of 'feel' during the build up of the pendulum cast, harshness and corrosion. Aluminium butts have a nasty habit of snapping in mid-cast because saltwater has eaten away the walls of the tube, but it is nothing that cannot be repaired with a new length of tube glued to the bottom of the rod. Most surf rods fitted with aluminium butts are very powerful and fast-actioned. Though not impossible for a beginner to master, they still present a few problems—mainly harshness and magnification of errors in style. When the choice falls between two equally good tip sections, one with a glass butt the other of aluminium, choose the former. If necessary you can always upgrade the rod by cutting off the glassfibre and glueing on a piece of alloy.

Line up all the glass/carbon, all-glass and glass/aluminium rods and blanks. Now check length.

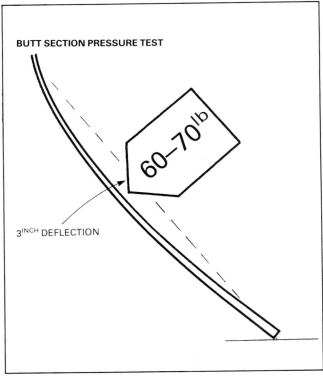

BUTT SECTION PRESSURE TEST

60–70^{lb}

3^{INCH} DEFLECTION

The butt pressure test—a simple method to determine the casting power of a beach rod.

Plain parallel handles with hosepipe clips are excellent for multiplier reel casting. The adjusting screw is a handy trigger for extra security.

Over the years, 11·5 feet has become the standard length for surf rods balanced to cast 5 ounces of lead, pendulum style. A few inches on top does not make much difference, so you should discard from the collection all those over 12 feet long or under 11·25 feet. It is a great mistake to take on more rod than you can handle. Too short a rod lacks power and feel, and is more difficult to time.

Now we are left with a handful of rods and blanks that are of the right materials, and either ideal length or close to it. Let us assess the blank (i.e. the tip and handle complete). It does not matter if the rod is made up of two equal-length sections or as long tip (usually about 8 feet long) plus detachable butt. Consider the whole unit at this stage. Put each rod together. Support the centre of the blank with your left hand and rest the butt on the ground. Now push down on the blank midway between left hand and floor. A firm shove with your right hand—say 50–70 lbs pressure—should flex that part of the rod some 3 inches. Discard all rods that flex like longbows under this test because they lack sufficient backbone for 5 ounce surfcasting. Make a note of those with butts so stiff that you cannot bend them more than an inch or so, however do not rule them out at this point. Although they are a little too rigid, they are far better than a soft rod. The chances are that a handful of rods and blanks pass this test with flying colours and that one of them is probably right for you.

The simple butt-pressure test is designed for powerful surfcasting tackle rather than freshwater rods and blanks. It can be modified to give a reasonable idea of the potential performance of lightweight surf and freshwater blanks as well. The formula for surf rods is used to calculate a ratio between hand pressure and casting weight. Divide the pressure necessary to flex the rod 3 inches out of line, by the sinker weight you intend to use. In the case of the surf rod just described, the figure works out to be 12—that is, 60 pounds divided by 5 ounces (forget the pounds and ounces). The factor 12 represents a stiffness ratio for a rod which casts extremly well (though not to tournament standards), but is still very nice to fish with. It will not explode baits, is light and sensitive and forgives many casting mistakes. Use that same factor to calculate the pressure for a lighter blank. Suppose you want a rod to cast 2 ounces. The pressure factor stays at 12, but this time you multiply by 2 instead of 5 to get hand pressure. In other words, a 24 pound push applied to the middle of the lower half of the blank, just as before, should produce a 3 inch flex.

The factor 12 is close to perfect for a beginner. Avoid rods which produce a factor of 10 (50 pounds pressure with 5 ounces, 20 pounds with 2 ounces) because they are just a little too soft in the butt to accommodate a hard pendulum cast. Go as high as 15 (75 and 30 pounds pressure for a 3 inch flex) without worrying whether the butt is too stiff. Full-power tournament blanks for 5–6 ounces will not bend 3 inches with less than 100 pounds and some you just cannot bend that far anyway. These ultra-stiff butts are too critical for a beginner and may even be too stiff for good fishing. Although sloppiness in the butt is impossible to live with whatever kind of caster you are, the stiffest rods do not necessarily produce better distances in surf. You cannot exploit their full potential without drilling yourself into the sand or smashing off baits. So overall, a factor of 12–15 should suit 99 per cent of all casters who practice on surf, lake, dam or river.

The rod butt provides leverage and resilience to drive the mid-section of the blank. The mid-section in turn accelerates sinker and terminal rig. The final 18–24 inches of the blank immediately below the tip ring help control that flow of power and also link the main part of the rod to sinker and shock leader. You should think of the end of the rod as being a flexible joint. These three zones of the complete blank determine the performance of a rod and complement the arc and power flow of the pendulum cast. Zoned action is fully described in another chapter, so for the moment all you need to know is how to identify a rod of that kind. The butt pressure test identifies all rods with a suitable zoned butt action. Now turn your attention to tip zones.

Outside diameter of the blank just below the tip ring should be approximately 1/8 inch. 3/16 inch is probably acceptable, but 1/4 inch or more rules out that blank altogether. Traditional surf men, particularly those brought up with American-style surf rods, always have initial reservations about such a flimsy tip, but they should not worry about it for the rod is nowhere near as underpowered as it seems. Fine diameter makes casting easier and actually protects the tip of the rod from overload. You cannot cast properly, pendulum style, with a large diameter, hard tip.

If the butt is right, and the tip diameter measures up to specification, it is almost inevitable that the mid-section of the blank is of correct wall thickness, taper rate and power. With thin diameter of upper blank and stiffness of butt virtually dictating upper and lower limits of the centre, that section cannot be too far off the mark whatever the precise design might be. There are subtle differences between rods with identical tip diameters and butt pressures, but as far as learning to cast is concerned, the individual characteristics of such blanks count for little. Later on you will probably come to like one type more than the rest, but by then you will know exactly what to look for anyway.

Two or three rods and blanks from the original selection in the shop will fit into the right category for pendulum surfcasting. You could confidently buy any of them; then feel, action and power would be very similar. At this stage you probably could not differentiate between them on that score. Which rod to buy depends on you. Do you want a ready-made beach rod, a kit or a bare blank? How much can you spend? Those are personal questions; but in my opinion it pays to check out fittings and accessories. You have several options.

All rods and blanks on your list are fundamentally sound as BLANKS go. Prices are likely to range between £25 and £90. Generally, you get what you pay for. Expensive tackle is better made and finished, and, if in rod form, has fittings and rings which will last a long time. An excellent rod is always a good investment. Even if you do not like it or soon outgrow it, secondhand value remains high. On the other hand, some would say that it makes more sense to buy a cheap but serviceable blank and build it for yourself. Another option, which I personally favour for anyone who does not want to go for a top-quality rod in the first place, is a cheap production rod. It is worth buying a good blank with poor rings, but only if the price is right. These days some of the better mass-production rods are actually cheaper than a bare blank. One rod, the Daiwa 5900, is well made and reasonably furnished, and with a good blank—quite a bargain at less than £30, and worth re-ringing if necessary. Of the other production rods, glassfibre ABU Atlantics are satisfactory, Fenwick Surf Sticks (with graphite butt and 'S' glassfibre tips) are superb. Daiwa and Fenwick are also available as bare blanks or part-built. The best pendulum blanks, apart from those two brands, are Conoflex and Carroll Zziplex. There are also a number of makers like Sportex, Pateke Morton, Fibatube and North Western who produce serviceable but generally uninspired blanks. Many blanks mentioned here are used by small manufacturers and custom builders like Going Brothers, Lite Rods, Ray Roberts, Simpsons of Turnford. American anglers should look through the Lamiglas saltwater range, which includes a few blanks suitable for lightweight pendulum casting.

All the blank jointing systems are satisfactory for routine beach casting. The Fenwick Feralite joint on this surf rod is particularly strong and reliable.

Handgrips spaced 30–32 inches apart encourage smooth, fast arm acceleration during the final flick of the cast.

34

Zoned Action Rods for Pendulum Casting

Modern casting rods capable of working baits and lures efficiently, playing big fish and casting to maximum range using the pendulum style, are designed to compromise between casting and fishing characteristics. Anglers brought up on old-fashioned slow action surf and spinning tackle nurse sore fingers and thumbs after trying the new breed of surf tackle. Pick up one of those stiff butt/whippy tip blanks and you are in trouble if you cast traditionally with a direct overhead thump. Even tournament casters suffer: the speed of blank is alien and does not react to casts that excel with through action rods and Hatteras Heavers.

Blanks and rods orignally produced for surf fishing and tournament casting in Britain, and now available in America and Europe, certainly do appear fast and powerful. But if you adopt a pendulum cast with its long sinker drop of at least 8 feet between sinker and rod tip, the rod feels ultra-smooth, precise and downright easy to handle. It is not unusual for a surf or freshwater angler to add 50–100 feet to his previous best cast and sometimes within minutes of changing tackle and technique. What is the secret formula? How can an experienced surf man who cast traditional tackle for twenty years be beaten by a newcomer in his first season on the beach?

Some call it cheating. And if exploiting space-age materials, less critical timing and lower physical effort does add up to bending rules, there are thousands of fishermen happy to live with it. Those who reach elusive fish 130–150 yards out in the surf or around the margins of a dam certainly never complain.

Who cares if you do not need years of practice to handle a multiplier (conventional) reel? On the new rods you set your reel to run freely on its bearings, with just a pair of small brake blocks or a magnetic controller to tame the initial surge of acceleration. Cast as hard as you like; tie on the weight of sinker or lure that best suits you and the fishing. The cast stays the same. Only minor alterations are necessary in sinker drop, timing and power flow. More to the point, just a couple of rods, light and heavy, master an entire range of baits and lures from ultra-light to heavy-duty surf.

Good pendulum blanks incorporate three distinct action zones which are married together in a single blank and handle. There is a flexible tip, powerful and responsive centre, and a stiff butt. No matter what length and casting weight the rod may be, design still conforms to this zoned, programmed action.

Zoned action blanks cast further for less effort. The same action formula also operates to your advantage when you work a lure, set the rod in a sandspike to detect bites, drive in the hook and fight a heavy fish. The blank cushions errors and insures line against snapping to a degree impossible with old-style rods. You cast better, detect more bites, and beat heavier fish on lighter tackle. It all adds up to more enjoyable sport.

ZONED-ACTION IN CLOSE-UP

Let us examine the structure of a typical 11·5 ft pendulum rod for casting 3–8 ounces. The same theory applies to all weights of high-performance tackle—freshwater and ultra-light surf rods are variations on the theme.

Zone A: The flexible tip of the blank is roughly 18–24 inches long and extends down from the tip guide to blend with the next zone. Extreme tip diameter is usually 1/8 in 'E' and 'S' glassfibre. Internal taper of the blank is quite slow—say 80 thousandths of an inch per foot on a multi-taper mandrel.

Zone B: The power zone lies in the centre of the bank, starts at the 18 inch limit of the tip and covers the next 72 inches of the rod. On most surf rods you will not detect any surface clues that herald the switch from ZONE A to B. Cheaper rods do not change internal taper anyway. Here the tip is flexible because blank walls and diameter are particularly thin at that point. Only advanced manufacturers like Fenwick-Woodstream have the technical ability to shift taper rates on the mandrel, which is the best method of building up the zones. However, better quality straight taper blanks are acceptable for most routine distance casting.

The power zone always features a medium-fast or fast taper rate which develops strength and blank speed progressively but rapidly within the centre section of the blank. Here casting power is loaded, stored and released during a pendulum cast. You need plenty of material to withstand pressure so the blank is usually around 1 inch diameter at the lower end of this zone, and may be reinforced with graphite.

Zone C: The leverage unit, approximately 42 inches of graphite, aluminium alloy tube or thick-walled fibreglass completes the blank. The Power Unit may be spigotted to the upper section of the rod, permanently jointed, or made detachable by the Feralite process, as on Fenwick's Surf Stick range.

Compared to a traditional surf rod, the butt of a modern pendulum rod is very stiff indeed and virtually unbendable on a powerful 5–8 ounce surf blank. Long 'S' or 'E' glass tips (zones A and B combined) plus detachable butt or spigotted handle are an ideal balance between materials technology, strength and performance.

HOW THE ZONES OPERATE DURING A PENDULUM CAST

Zones work both independently and in unison from the initial pendulum swing of lure or sinker until moments after line is released. Let us stop the cast in stages and analyse power transfer.

Diagram 1: The preliminary outswing of the sinker on its leader drop should be slow but still hard enough to lift the sinker to at least eye level. Zones B and C form a solid foundation for the tip, Zone A, which flexes gently. Zoned action buffers a pendulum swing against slight mistakes in timing and direction and generally smooths the start of a cast. It is extremely difficult to control an extended pendulum swing on a stiff-tipped blank.

Diagram 2: A gentle push down with the left hand transmits enough tip speed through the butt and centre zones to flip the sinker into its backswing. Again, only Zone A flexes.

Diagram 3: As the caster's body begins to rotate, the sinker tries to maintain its position at the peak of the pendulum inswing. Its inertia draws Zone A into compression and then directs power down into Zone B. All you actually feel is a slight resistance between the handgrips—as if you were pulling the rod along its length, javelin style. As body rotation progresses and builds more power and speed into the cast, Zone B begins to work hard. The more you load it, the more it bends.

Diagram 4: Shoulders swing around to face almost squarely towards the sea. Muscle strength pours from legs, waist and back, and is channelled into Zone B by way of the upper tip. The harder the cast and the heavier a sinker and bait, the more Zone B is compressed and loaded. The tip zone, A, is actually bypassed and STRAIGHTENS TO FORM A LOOSE LINK BETWEEN THE LEADER AND THE CENTRE ZONE OF THE BLANK.

Now you feel stiffness and resilience between your hands. Having soaked up its full complement of bend and workload, the upper blank channels extra power and speed directly to the stiff butt. As you punch and pull with your arms you should notice that the rod feels 'locked'—is unable to bend any more and thus becomes a solid lever. Lock-up point is a critical factor in rod design and extends beyond surf tackle to boat, fly and freshwater casting.

There is a paradox here. The sensation you feel during a good cast is of power being fed DOWN the rod, towards you. The tip loads, Zone B flexes and locks, then the butt stiffens between your hands. In fact, power is transmitted UP the rod, while inertia of the sinker provides an opposing force. It is important to understand that despite this clash with pure physics, that is how a rod should actually feel in mid cast. I stress the point because, during a bad cast, power really does seem to flow upwards from your hands all through the cast. It is an obscure phenomenon that good casters take for granted and poor performers never experience, and concerns the mechanics of making a rod 'work', an exercise described in the casting section of the book.

Diagram 5: At the precise moment of line release, the unyielding butt zone magnifies and directs the final power surge and acceleration of Zone B. The middle of the blank unleashes a massive propulsive force, but it is *smooth and controlled* and nothing like the haphazard response of a traditional surf rod. As Zone B flicks straight, Zone A recompresses slightly, adding a marginal boost to sinker speed, ironing out minor errors in the cast.

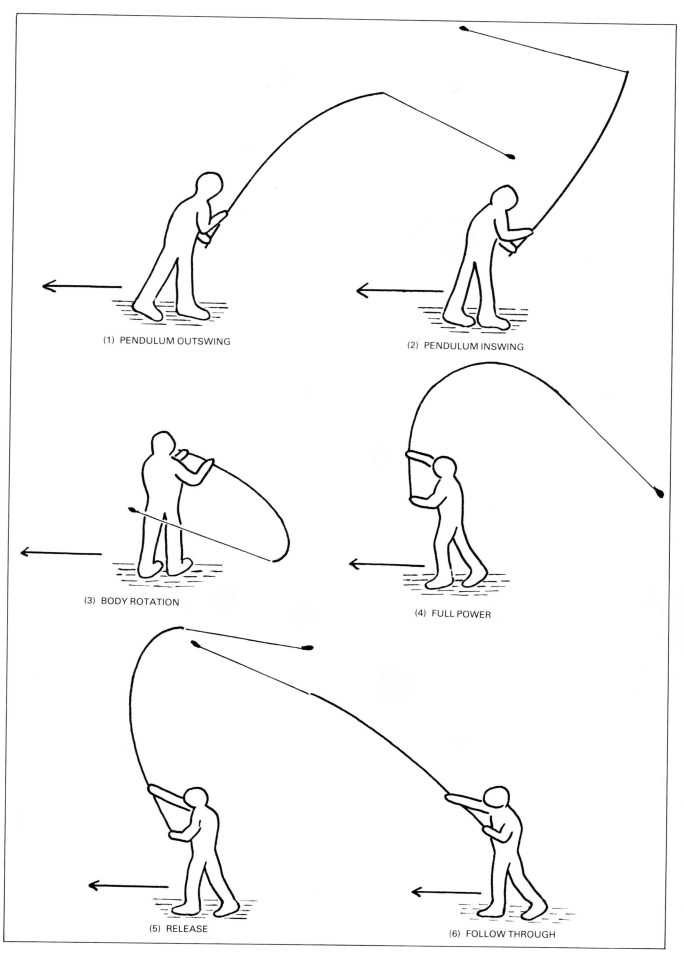

(1) PENDULUM OUTSWING

(2) PENDULUM INSWING

(3) BODY ROTATION

(4) FULL POWER

(5) RELEASE

(6) FOLLOW THROUGH

Diagram 6: Zones B and C are now relaxed, straight and virtually stationary. Zone A follows through to maintain smoothness and control, an important phase which helps eliminate backlash on a multiplier reel and eases the passage of leader knot through rings. The tip is so light and responsive that it straightens and stops dead. Heavy-tipped blanks oscillate for a long time which is a distinct hazard to multiplier control, and often the cause of leader knots wrapping around the rings.

Once you master a pendulum cast and have tuned your reel to the blank, you will discover that something like 30 per cent of the effort previously expended in casting an old-fashioned rod 80 yards now produces 120 yards or more. Modern blank action, along with full power drawn from legs, waist and shoulders, reduces the load on your arms by an almost unbelievable amount. It can be calculated that the reward for effort ratio of a zoned blank is vastly superior. About 45 per cent of the power intake of a Hatteras Heaver is wasted because of the rod's inherent mechanical limitations, further restricted by heavy control necessary to keep a multiplier from backlashing. Pendulum casting with a zoned blank transfers around 90 per cent of your muscle input to the sinker. Minimal reel control, and, if you like, lighter running line on the spool, sponge up only a fraction of the sinker's available kinetic energy. You cast farther, more easily and with full confidence.

THE FISHING QUALITIES OF ZONED ACTION BLANKS

Zoned-action blanks are equally good for working lures, detecting tiny bites at long range and for battling strong fish in heavy water. The same programmed sections of blank that smooth the cast and release full body power still operate when the bait is in the water but in reverse.

Zone A: The tip of the blank is so sensitive to line vibration that you feel the slightest bite. With the rod in a sandspike and line pulled tight between sinker and tip ring, Zone A flexes and remains compressed against the pull of wind and tide. Pre-stressed, the tip irons out wind and wave movement—which may signal false bites—and picks up tremors you would not notice on an ordinary rod.

Super-sensitive bite detection is not necessary all the time, but there are many occasions in surf and freshwater when a fish takes bait so gently you feel nothing. Those are the days you wind in to find bait gone. Maybe it really was crabs and shrimps . . . could be it was a sneaky cod or bass. Some of the biggest fish are hardest to detect: a 20

pound-plus cod in Britain's winter surf will sometimes flicker the rod tip just a couple of inches. On a zoned rod you can feel six inch flounders chew a bait 500 feet out in rough water. If anything, tip sensitivity is too high for beginners who snatch the rod at the slightest sign of life.

Zone B: The centre of the rod is progressively powerful and stiff. As you strike the fish, the bend of the rod gradually transfers from Zone A to B. The harder you and the fish work out, the more of B is brought into play. Lower sections of the rod start to work while the very tip is gradually bypassed.

Traditional heavy surf rods have a narrow power band. The blank does little until line tension is high. A pendulum rod responds to very small tip pressures, yet still has the backbone to haul on 25–40 lb test line when necessary. More 'feel' is transmitted down to the handle. The rod greatly improves response time of the reel's drag plates.

Wide power band and its built-in cushion mean you can afford to push yourself and the tackle to their limits without risking a snapped line. You can either kill fish quickly on heavy line or reduce breaking strain and go for pure sport, along with a significant increase in casting range.

Zone C: The rigid butt (rigid on a surf rod, that is—lighter rods do have more flexibility to accommodate lower line test and smaller casting weights) is a solid lever for you to work against. There is nothing more disconcerting than a butt which 'gives' under your hands when power is turned on. There is input to consider as well: a stiff, light handle, especially graphite, transmits every tremor and change in line pressure as they run down the line and through the blank. You sense the lure working through the water and can almost visualise a fish grate its teeth on the hooks. Monitoring line pressure during the fight is ten times more precise on a zoned rod. In all, the stiff butt adds up to enhanced control.

Zoned action rods—the popular questions

Why do these rods rip the skin off my thumb when I cast traditionally?
The blank is designed to load and release its power over a long, smooth arc. If you cast overhead-style, the blank part-loads then releases like lightning and you just cannot control it.

Why doesn't that flimsy tip snap off?
Zone A cannot overload enough to break off unless you abuse the rod. When it encounters

Zoned blanks won't operate with old-style casting methods. Pendulum cast and an exaggerated sinker drop are important— the drop is the MINIMUM for smooth results with 5 ounces of lead.

The tip section is extremely sensitive to bites. When line is pulled taut against the inertia of a grip-wired sinker, you can feel the smallest of fish at long distance.

A split second before line release: the powerful mid-section unleashes its force while the flexible tip buffers the cast from errors. The top 18 inches of blank reduce backlash on multipliers.

Powerful Zone B exerts full pressure on a heavy fish. A good zoned blank balanced for 5 ounce casting handles lines between 12 and 35 lb test.

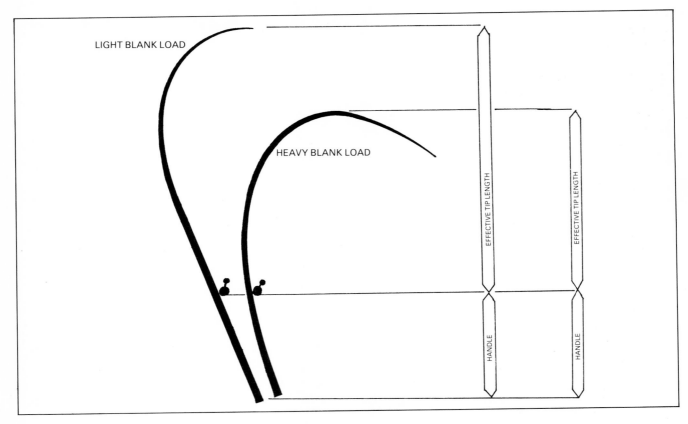

LIGHT BLANK LOAD

HEAVY BLANK LOAD

EFFECTIVE TIP LENGTH

EFFECTIVE TIP LENGTH

HANDLE

HANDLE

too much stress, whether from casting or fishing, the blank automatically shifts load from Zone A to B. It may look downright cruel to pendulum cast 8 ounces and half a mackeral on a ⅛ inch diameter tip, but it is perfectly safe and easier than on a thick tip.

Why not cut off the tip anyway?

Zone A is a vital link between the main power-house of the rod, line and fish/sinker. Just 18 inches of flexible glassfibre blended to a progressive middle and butt make a vast difference to handling and performance. You notice enhanced smoothness and control, freedom from backlash and supreme bite detection. Zone A is an inbuilt computer which does a lot of the thinking for you.

How can the same blank handle such a wide sinker range—say, 3 to 8 ounces on a surf model?

Because it is many rods in one. The harder you cast and the greater the sinker load, the more you compress Zones A and B. Zone B is quickly bypassed, straightens out, then follows through during the main power stroke of a pendulum cast. You 'dial in' lower sections of rod and utilise the rigidity of butt for leverage.

In contrast, a light sinker is flicked away by the flexible tip and upper section of Zone B. The diagram shows how a pendulum rod com-pensates for light and heavy loads. You see how the rod effectively shortens as pressures and load increase? You cast 3 ounces on an effective 11·5 feet, 5 ounces on the lower 10 feet, 8 ounces on the bottom 8 feet, by which time Zone A and a small part of Zone B are bypassed. Given a constant distance between your hands, effective reduction in tip length raises mechanical advantage in your favour. You cast a heavy sinker as easily as a small one. Timing and speed of cast vary, but sensation of power flow is relatively unchanged between sinker weights.

By the same token, the blank exploits a wider range of line tests: say, 12–40 lb on a heavy-duty surf model. The harder you and the fish pull, the more the leverage ratio swings in your favour. Set the reel's drag to protect line, and you are unlikely to snap off even if the fish momentarily gets the better of you.

Which is better—multiplier or spinning (fixed spool) reel?

It makes no difference to a zoned action rod since timing the cast is the same for each reel. Multipliers require no special tuning, spool thumbing or over-tightening of bearing caps. You need never touch the spool from release to splash down. A zoned rod is a marvellous confidence builder for surf men who have always dreamed of mastering the multiplier reel but never could.

Rod Materials and Blank Design

Zoned action blanks offer the best casting performance along with good fishing characteristics. Glassfibre rods are perfectly adequate for most surf fishing and long-range freshwater applications. On the face of it, then, there is no need to look deeper into either materials or alternative designs of blanks. If you aim to learn pendulum technique, the zoned blank theory and the guide to choosing a suitable rod are everything you need to know about rod design. However, the more involved angler likes to understand carbon fibre, alternative actions and lengths of rods. New materials and specialised blanks really do help develop more advanced fishing methods, and they may offer significant improvements in distance with lightweight plugs and lures. Argument for lighter tackle grows stronger as quality of fishing generally deteriorates. To exploit 8 lb test nylon instead of standard 12–15 lb surf line, action and power of rod must be altered, otherwise the line will snap on almost every cast. At the moment you might not need a 13 foot surf rod. Next year, however, your casting could benefit and you may possibly want to enter distance tournaments, where the extra 15 yards provided by a longer blank could help you set new World Records.

GLASSFIBRE

As a material for rod building, glassfibre offers a good blend of performance, sensitivity and cost. The vast majority of surf and casting rods for weights over 2 ounces are still glassfibre despite the rapid advance of more exotic blanks in freshwater lure and fly fishing. Glassfibre in an easy material to manufacture, store and work. Simple mandrels produce a variety of actions, and to build in more power you can thicken the walls a little which is a cheap way to upgrade existing designs.

Glassfibre is unquestionably the best material for your first casting rod. Provided the blank is zoned, adequately powerful and the correct length, there is no reason why you should settle for less than 175 yards. Many an old glassfibre blank still churns out a steady stream of 225 yard casts. I, for example, have a 12 year-old ABU 464 Conolon blank which has stiffened a little with age and now casts farther than when brand new. The Bruce and Walker SX406 is another obsolescent rod that stands well alongside modern high-performance blanks.

Yes, modern bottom and mid-market glassfibre rods are fairly primitive but any blank which passes the tip and hand pressure tests outlined elsewhere in the book will cast well enough for learning to cast pendulum style. But the blank is not as sensitive, lively and powerful as highest-grade glassfibre. With prices ranging upward of £20 for a blank or £30 for a built rod, you cannot really expect much more for your money. You may outgrow the rod, learn to hate its weight and bad balance, or curse it every time a ring breaks off, but you still learned to cast 150 yards or more and the investment paid off.

The economics of manufacturing rods and blanks is fast polarising the industry: mass-production in the Far East undercuts high labour costs in Europe and America and the West simply cannot compete at the cheaper end of the market. The result is that more and more glassfibre rods are imported. The bulk of them are mediocre—as far as long-casting is concerned—yet there are a few that pass tests outlined in the section 'Choosing a rod'.

Blank makers can still afford to pour realistic design and quality into ordinary 'E' glassfibre. Custom rod builders turn out reasonable surf rods. You can make up your own casting rod. It is in mass-production that standards are lower, and falling. The writing is on the wall: low-cast glassfibre rods for long-distance work are obsolescent, and blanks will follow.

'S' grade glassfibre is quite different from ordinary rod material. It is faster, lighter, more sensitive and of significantly better casting potential. In many respects it rivals carbonfibre for surf and heavy casting rods. Add its amazing toughness and lower price, and you have a material which presently outstrips carbon in the race towards the perfect all-round surf blank. The drawback is

41

manufacturing technology: 'S' glassfibre does not give its best performance without advanced design, very careful manufacture and multi-tapered mandrels. Fenwick Woodstream are the only company to fully exploit theoretical advantages of 'S' glass for surf work and lighter freshwater distance. Surf Sticks are in a class of their own—the only zoned action, high-performance blanks and rods on the market.

CARBON FIBRE

This space-age material is even faster, lighter and better casting than 'S' glass. Specialised raw materials for the tackle industry are more advanced than cloth employed in the first carbonfibre rods, which were unreliable, to say the least. The remaining bugbear is price—very few surf men are prepared to invest in a blank which costs at least three times as much as good glass.

Actually, that is a blinkered view. Carbonfibre holds the key to the future of surf and general distance casting. It does cast farther for the same effort, handles lighter lines, enhances bite detection and weighs far less. In a word, carbonfibre is precise – to a degree impossible to achieve in glassfibre. BUT, that very precision imposes extra responsibilities on the angler. He too must be specific – must select a rod for a range of sinker weights and line tests, of exact action and length and for a particular style of casting. A 'normal' glass surf rod should handle 4–8 ounces of lead, 12–40 lb line, allow reasonable results with any efficient casting style, and be tolerant of an angler's exact length and action requirements. A top-grade carbon beach rod may cast 4-ounces on 10–12 lb line with a fishing pendulum cast. At 12 feet long, it would not suit a man whose physique is better matched to 11 feet. Parameters are strict; though of course it is possible to design a rod for virtually any combination of sinker weight, action, line test and style. Anglers who dabbled in carbonfibre with poor results usually chose inferior grade blanks and failed to narrow down the specifications. This material trades off superior performance against diminished versatility.

Glassfibre rods are highly recommended to beginners because they will handle such a range of tackle and can accommodate stresses which inevitably occur when you are learning to cast. A pendulum cast that loses control and direction can savagely twist the blank through two or three opposing planes. Carbonfibre will not forgive these mistakes, and the cast is sure to go astray. The rod may eventually pull itself apart if the error is ingrained in the caster's style.

Design and materials specification are critical in modern surf rods. Jim Bruce, of Bruce & Walker, checks out a sample of carbon fibre before cutting it to shape for the mandrel.

Wrapping and taping the raw material to the mandrel before curing the blank. Blank quality is dependant on careful workmanship.

42

Suppose, after mastering a pendulum style, you settle on 5 ounces of lead, 12 lb test main line, multiplier reel and a 12 foot rod and you normally cast 125 yards (the ideal distance for the beaches you fish) would carbon fibre add to your expertise?

A carbon blank weighs about half as much as a glassfibre one. The action is sweeter yet somehow more powerful—a difficult characteristic to define and typical of the finest carbon rods. Either you would cast the same distances with noticeably less effort, or the same casting power as before would add another 10–15 yards. Another alternative is to choose a slightly slower blank action with a few pounds less pressure on the butt (see the hand pressure detailed elswhere) which would retain the casting distance of the old glass rod but allow you to cast much softer baits. This could well be the deciding factor if you fish a lot with peeler crab or shrimp, which are notoriously difficult to throw a long way unless they are wrapped up in shearing elastic or even frozen to the trace. The cast would be even more protected from backlash—carbon fibre delivers its power and acceleration more progressively than glass.

Bite sensitivity is in a class of its own. You would almost certainly need to rethink your fishing style, otherwise you could easily spend all day striking at bites from crabs and tiny fish too small to swallow bait. A good carbon blank is so light at the tip (and lightness counts more than pure flexibility in bite detection) that even a sinker shifting a few inches in the current is clearly signalled. Advantage goes beyond bites: as you reel in, the blank transmits every last vibration to your hands. A good carbon rod feels change of seabed as the sinker rolls along—you sense a clear difference between sand, mud and shingle even at 150 yards-plus. When you fight a big fish, carbonfibre completely outclasses glassfibre. Overall, the RIGHT carbon rod is so much better that you would never want to fish again with a glass surf blank.

Versatility is more important for anglers who travel to different beaches, fish for a variety of species, or who must sometimes change the sinker weight to suit the prevailing weather conditions. Those considerations tip the balance back to glassfibre for general surf fishing. One alternative for the non-specialist is a set of carbonfibre rods . . . but that is a very big investment. Another would be to use a glass rod for all-round sport and one or two carbons for the fishing you enjoy most.

I use an 'S' glass tip/graphite butt surf rod for its versatility: I cast 3–8 ounces on a range of lines, with all kinds of baits and tackle. This is the rod for conger eels, flatfish, bluefish, channel bass and cod. I could take it medium-heavyweight surfcasting anywhere in the world confident in its ability to cast well and handle whatever species I hooked. If I have room for only one rod, that is the one for me unless I am going to fish for a single species in unique conditions.

I greatly enjoy light fishing—lines down to 6 lb test, sinkers less than 4 ounces, and here I switch to a 12 or 13 foot carbon rod specially designed and built for this kind of fishing. It far outperforms the 'S' glass tip, casts extremely well with such small weights and feels ten times more sensitive and better balanced. I can easily justify the cost; and, in fact, I could argue that unless I owned these rods, I could not fish this way at all.

I also have a 13·75 foot rod for casting 5–5·5 ounces on heavy shock leader and 0·35 mm tournament grade line. It is invaluable for casting over grass for pure distance, and for blasting out a bait to spring cod which, in my part of the world, are shy of clear, sunlit water. Without bait close to 175 yards out from the surfline I am not likely to hook a fish all day. Again the special qualities of carbonfibre are worth the expense: the rod blank weighs just 12 ounces, is deceptively powerful and smooth to cast, yet handles relatively light lines with safety. Bite detection is superb – a prerequisite for fishing at these extreme ranges. I could get acceptable results with the 'S' glass rod but for me it is a personal preference to fish carbonfibre in these conditions.

SEMI-CARBON

Combining a limited amount of carbonfibre cloth in a standard glassfibre blank produces a hybrid casting rod with high performance coupled to versatility and reasonable price. Usually carbon reinforces the lower part of the tip section beginning just above the handle joint and extends between 3 and 5 feet towards the tip ring.

Carbonfibre used this way has only one advantage of any significance: it stiffens a rod without adding surplus mass or diameter. Take a standard glassfibre medium-fast or fast actioned blank that runs out of steam at 200 yards, wrap a chunk of stiff carbon around the lower half of the tip section, and you boost the range of 225 yards or more—simply by preventing blank overload at that stress point. The very tip of the rod remains flexible, which in glassfibre design terms means it is still able to detect bites, handle a range of sinkers and line tests, and will not explode baits unless power is turned on fully. It is a compromise blanks, they have none of the major handling bonuses of pure carbon, nor are they any better than a good 'S' glass tip. In the long term there is some problem with delamination of carbon from the glassfibre of the main blank. The wide variation of modulus between glass and carbon, plus the limitations of the resin matrix that binds the fibres together, encourages the rod to literally tear itself apart.

On the whole, though, a good semi-carbon is a better rod than an 'E' glass surfcaster. The beginner is still advised to stick to a glass rod, or an 'S' tip with a graphite butt. That is because most semi-carbons are designed for high-power casting and, like all high-performance rods, are critical of technique and tackle tuning. They also exaggerate the tendancy of all good casting rods to have a MINIMUM casting range. Unless you can exceed a lower limit of power, the rod will simply not work. Sub-100 yard casters beware!

Butt materials

Many of today's surf and long range casting rods are manufactured as long tips and short butts. The typical format is an 8·5 foot tip spigotted or Feralite-jointed to a handle long enough to bring total rod length up the desired 11·5–12 feet. Some rods are permanently spliced together at the butt, then cut and spigotted in the middle for easier transportation and storage. Either stystem is good, but diehard surfmen prefer a detachable butt and one-piece tip.

Glassfibre blanks may have aluminium alloy, graphite or glassfibre butts, usually in parallel tube form. Glass butts are acceptable for long distance work although they tend to run out of steam beyond 175 yards; by then walls and diameter are so great (for stiffness) that the handle is too thick to grip and so heavy it unbalances the whole rod. In the lower ranks of distance, glass butts are excellent for their 'feel' and forgiveness of error. Beginners like them very much.

Aluminium alloy adds stiffness without weight. Stiffness is important with a high-power glass tip and cannot be compromised on semi-carbons and some all-carbon tips. One inch diameter, 16SWG wall high-tensile aluminium drives an 11·5 foot surf rod to new performance levels. It may bend if used on longer rods cast with more than 5 ounces. Here 1·125 inch diamter or more, same wall thickness and alloy specification, answers the needs of the best casters and anglers. The snag with aluminium is loss of 'feel'. Absolute rigidity takes its toll of bad casts and poor style.

Carbon fibre tubular butts are the only serious choice for carbon tips although aluminium alloy

Just at the point of locking-up in mid-cast, a zoned action rod stiffens under the caster's hands in a smooth surge of leverage and acceleration. Soft butts are useless for this style of long range fishing.

which opens up the tournament field and perhaps makes life on the beach a little more successful in terms of distance and control. However, though these semi-carbons are better than some 'E' glass

Medium-fast, lightweight action blanks are fine for lure work. The correct zoned-action blank throws a small metal lure well over 100 yards on 10 lb line.

Brute power is the key to some forms of beachcasting. Conger eel fishing into deep water obstructed by rocks and weeds requires a robust rod with the design emphasis more on retrieve power than on sheer distance.

handles are acceptable as far as performance goes, but ruin the balance and lightness of carbon—factors which head the reasons to buy carbon in the first place. Carbon tube is immensely valuable on 'S' glass and semi-carbon tips as well. It is a beautifully powerful material and at least as powerful as alloy. The real advantage is increased tip acceleration and 'feel'.

Carbon fibre has the ideal characteristic of bending a little, then locking solid. You notice a much smoother power load in the cast, and the sinker gets away considerably faster. Locked carbon tube unleashes powerful spring-like acceleration when you release the line. Unlike the 'dead' drive of rigid alloy, carbon imparts the same leverage PLUS a final boost—almost an afterburn effect which rockets tackle skyward. You can measure the extra performance—smoother casts, less backlash with reels tuned to the limit, and around 10 per cent more distance than with an alloy butt and 20 per cent more than with plain glassfibre.

It is possible that boron fibres will add even more butt performance to surf rods and spinning tackle. Experiments show that a stiff boron butt is even slimmer than carbonfibre, and is thus easier to hold (which in itself adds more sting to the

cast). However, cost is prohibitive right now. Other alternatives loom on the edges of rod design. New generation plastics, among them advanced polycarbonates, might offer stiff, lively butts at relatively low cost. At the moment, choose carbonfibre if you can justify the extra expense. The standard you cast is unimportant—the material adds distance, precision and control to any surf tip. Beginners and experienced anglers cast better and enjoy their fishing even more.

OTHER BLANK ACTIONS

A fast, zoned action blank with stiff butt is superior for everyday long distance fishing with lures and baits. Most surf and freshwater anglers are happy to remain loyal to the design, which has proved itself over millions of fish on thousands of beaches, lakes and rivers. In more specialised fishing you can switch designs with advantage.

A slower action blank without quite as much butt power relative to tip speed (say a stiffness factor of 8–10) is perfect for casting baits and artificials, which by virtue of their specific gravity and shape cannot cast a long way, no matter how hard you try, or are so soft that a modest cast on a stiff zoned-action rod tears them to shreds.

45

Crabs are an excellent example of baits which cannot be cast a long way unless bound to the hook with a maze of elasticated thread. Some fish are happy to eat such bait, others, like shy-feeding bass in rocky ground, will not touch them unless appearance also is right. A soft rod lobs crab plenty far enough, whereas the standard surf rod either smashes the bait or is difficult to control. (All high-performance blanks, zoned models too, suffer to some degree from control loss on short range casts which do not allow the blank to operate as it should.) A slower rod may begin to 'work' really well at 75 yards range. Crab fishing for bass is almost exclusively a short-range sport, so you gain nothing by using a rod with high-performance capability.

Plug baits—especially surface lures and poppers—are extremely hard to cast a long way. You can hit the cast as hard as you like, but the bait is so light and bulky that it simply cannot tolerate so much acceleration and speed. A slightly less powerful butt and softer mid-action produce casts which fall within 90 per cent of those possible with the most powerful casting weapon, and with much less effort and greater control. A plug rod roughly conforming to zoned action still outcasts a standard sloppy-actioned surf or freshwater rod. A return to old-style surf and freshwater blanks is not the answer.

Fixed spool casters may benefit from a slightly heavier tip zone. Stiffness and additional power are irrelevant, although you may need them to compensate for specialised rod rings preferred by some casters. Slight extra weight in the tip helps smooth line flow immediately after release and resolves the eternal headache of leader knots and line tangles which always seem to accompany high-power fixed spool work.

Heavier tip plus three or four weighty, large diameter rings spaced well up the rod are one way to improve fixed spool casting. Another method is to soften the mid-section by around 15 per cent while boosting the top two feet by a few sixteenths of an inch in diameter. Then you can use a set of lighter but still moderately large diameter rings set evenly along the tip. Spanish casters, who excel with fixed spool reels, favour a quite soft action rod with a limited zone action, BUT they make up for lower efficiency in the blank by raising its length beyond 14 feet. The enhanced cushioning action of such a long rod also permits better casting and safer fishing with very light lines. As a general rule, whatever type of fishing you prefer, use progressively softer and longer rods in step with a decrease in line test.

ROD LENGTH

Everyone develops pet ideas about fishing tackle. No two anglers agree on every aspect of tackle, but on rod length for all-round surf fishing a concensus does arise. 11·5 feet seems perfect for most anglers casting pendulum style with 3–8 ounce zoned action rods.

It is highly unlikely that 11·5 feet will seriously hamper your attempts to learn good casting. Another rod may add distance, but initially that is not the issue at stake. You need the best possible chance to master the skills of pendulum cast and reel control. Statistically, it seems you are more likely to get the best results with an 11·5 foot surf blank. I strongly advise you not to stray under 11 feet or over 12 until you know exactly how to assess rod length as it applies to you personally.

No matter how well you cast, the direct rewards of modified rod length are hard to measure from the surf. You will not cast a bait significantly farther. Even if your casts with baits averaged ten yards more, only once or twice a year would that show an extra fish in the bag. Long rods are generally no more senstive to bites, nor does the tip hold line farther away from surf and backwash—at least, not far enough to make any real difference to wave action's effect on the rod tip. Longer rods are actually slightly less efficient at hauling in big fish. Shorter rods do not make casting any easier with heavy sinkers, even though theorectically they should. The more common result of shortening the rod from 11·5 feet is to exaggerate timing mistakes in pendulum swing and power arc.

Those observations are aimed at normal casting with standard surf tackle. You do not need such a long rod with the lighter weights. 10 feet is perfectly acceptable with 2–4 ounce lures; 9·25 feet balances nicely to ⅝–1 ounce, (although you can use a longer, lighter rod if you like) and as we have seen in relation to light line casting, a rod longer than 11·5 feet is fine with as much as 4–5 ounces, provided you compensate for extra length with a slower taper and less backbone.

In pure distance terms—almost specifically in tournament casting terms—you should experiment with longer surf rods. Basically, there are two types of caster: slow and fast. A slow, average strength man gets his best results with an 'average' 11·5 foot rod whilst a slow but extremely strong caster can afford to lengthen his rod. He has the necessary muscle to swing the beast. Sinker speed is produced by generating high tip speed in the rod. There are two ways to arrive at the same result: a long rod moved slowly, or a short one

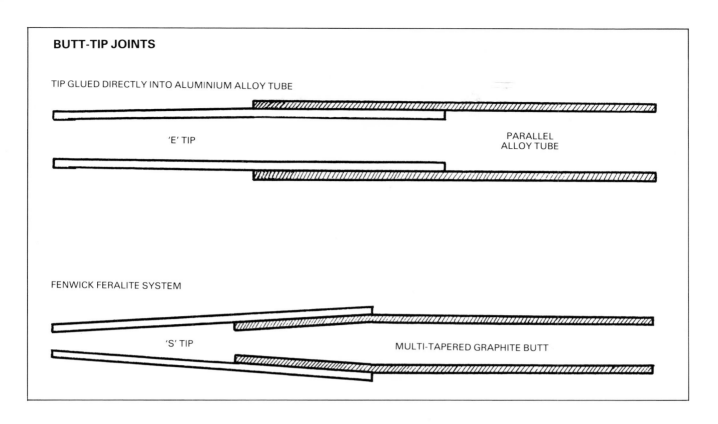

BUTT-TIP JOINTS

TIP GLUED DIRECTLY INTO ALUMINIUM ALLOY TUBE

'E' TIP

PARALLEL ALLOY TUBE

FENWICK FERALITE SYSTEM

'S' TIP

MULTI-TAPERED GRAPHITE BUTT

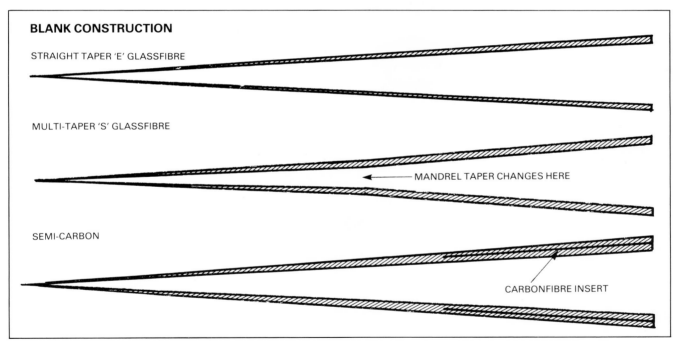

BLANK CONSTRUCTION

STRAIGHT TAPER 'E' GLASSFIBRE

MULTI-TAPER 'S' GLASSFIBRE

MANDREL TAPER CHANGES HERE

SEMI-CARBON

CARBONFIBRE INSERT

moved quickly. It takes more physical effort to push a big and inevitably heavier rod, which is also fighting air pressure as it rotates through the casting arc. A strong man who cannot move fast uses a longer rod to generate the same tip speed as a faster, less powerful caster who can really swish a short blank but is unable to do half as well with, say, a 13·5 foot blank.

The theory works well. Slow, powerful casters really do benefit from an extra couple of feet. If you fit this category, make a few tests—the results might be an extra 20 yards. The perfect caster would be both fast and powerful—strong enough to handle a long rod and fast enough to bring it through at the same speed as a shorter rod. With such qualities record casts are made. It is no coincidence that many leading British and South African tournament casters use long rods. The winners are big, fast men in a sport that is becoming the stronghold of the athlete angler.

Rods Rings and Fittings

ROD RINGS

It pays to invest in the best rod rings (guides). Many a good rod is ruined by cheap rings which reduce distances, strain the blank and chew line to pieces. The reverse is also true: a mediocre blank upgrades into an acceptable fishing rod by whipping on a set of top-quality rings. Check your surf rod to see exactly how the rings affect the bend and power of the blank. You might cast 20 yards farther by repositioning the intermediates. Moving the butt ring a foot farther away from a fixed spool reel reduces wind knots and trapped leaders.

Rod rings share two responsibilities: they correctly align leader with the compressed blank and they form a tunnel for inward and outward line flow. The right set of rings, correctly positioned on the blank, helps wring the ultimate performance from fixed spool and multiplier reels, each of which requires a specific ring pattern for peak results. However, it is not strictly necessary to switch to a special fixed spool or multiplier rod until your distances exceed 175 yards. Even 200 yard casts are easily accommodated on rods ringed for both reels. In fact, the surf angler who selects reels according to beach conditions usually prefers a rod that casts nicely with both. It makes sense to use versatile tackle when you can—and of course it is cheaper to have one rod instead of two.

Rings for multiplier casting. The zoned action surf rod, 11·5 feet long and matched to 0·35–0.40 mm diameter main line, probably requires at least six intermediate rings. Ideally, the number of rings should be cut to the bare minimum that spreads the load of casting and fishing over the full working length of glass or carbonfibre. Tournament casters sometimes prefer the same pattern even if it results in limited contact between line and blank when the rod is under full compression with a fish on the hook. Flexibility of the tip two feet of a pendulum blank fished with the reel on top of the handle certainly encourages line to hang in chords between rings.

In my experience you should balance theoretically correct ring spacing, which prevents line touching the blank, against weight saved by cutting out one or two rings near the top of the rod. I have never found that it has made any difference to the rod if line did make contact here and there. I have not lost any fish through friction burns. As long as you do not allow great gaps between rings, and therefore overload the blank unnecessarily, the rod never suffers.

By whipping, say, three rings instead of four on the top zone of the blank, some rods cast more smoothly. The more sensitive the blank tip to excessive weight, the more important it is to reduce ring size and numbers, even at risk of losing perfect line flow along the rod. There is no single formula to calculate the best ring spacings and numbers on this or any other fishing rod. Tape on a set of rings, then cast and fish until trial and error determines the best compromise.

Where rings are closely spaced on a flexible tip to preserve blank action, choose small, lightweight rings. If the tip is stiffer, which makes it less sensitive to extra weight and fairly immune to line drop between the rings, you have the option of whipping on three or four large diameter, high-standing rings like the Fuji BSHGs, or five or six low-set, smaller diameter rings—Fuji BNHG, Seymo or Daiwa Dynaflo. Use which one you prefer, but remember that small rings soon clog with weed.

The mid-section of the blank (Zone B) does not flex enough to bring line into contact. Use as few rings as necessary to spread the load. Some rods need only two rings—but if you are in doubt, add another for luck. This zone of the rod is so stiff that the weight of one more ring will not be noticed. The lowest ring—the butt ring which collects line directly from the reel—should be at least 25 mm in diameter. 30 mm is better if you use 40 pound-plus shock leader. Height of ring also aids line flow. Ideally its centre should be at spool level so that the line neither rises nor dives into the ring. BSHG rings may be better than BSHG-type for large capacity reels like the ABU 9000C and Penn 970. Aim to have around 30 inches minimum between reel and butt ring regardless of ring and spool dimensions.

Rings for fixed spool casting. A fixed spool is fished under the rod. The line never drifts close to the blank when the rod is pulled heavily on a fish. In fact the opposite may occur—line creeps too far from the blank and jumps in such big chords between rings that the blank is not correctly loaded. This is a particular hazard on fixed spool rods fitted with three or four rings only, all whipped on the upper half of the blank.

The idea of a few, large diameter rings is to eliminate line friction and to prevent the leader knot catching in the butt ring or tip immediately after line release on a powerful cast. In general the scheme works well but it can strain the tip. Tournament casters use a slightly stiffer tip to support the extra weight and torsion of the rings, and to produce a smoother line delivery. A typical high-performance surf rod between 11 and 12 feet long, used with the reel in the high butt position, would feature a 16 mm tip ring, 20, 30, 40 and 50 mm intermediates on the top 6 feet of the blank, and a gap of at least 40 inches between the 50 mm ring and the reel. Line flow is excellent, yet the rod still fishes quite well. Fuji BSHG rings are universally accepted for fixed spool work, chiefly because they sit nice and high off the blank.

Space between reel spool and butt ring is more critical than any other dimension in fixed spool ringing. Without an appreciable free-flow area before the shock leader passes into the butt ring, the chances of a tangle escalate; a butt ring 18 inches from the spool traps the leader every cast. Under no circumstances should you reduce the gap below 30 inches.

One school of thought says that the butt ring should be small to break up the coned flow of line leaving a spool. The idea has merit, but few surf anglers travel that road. The alternative philosophy—to whip on large diameter rings to reduce friction—is still popular. The friction side of the argument is not watertight: in either case direct ring friction is minimal on surf tackle. What counts is lack of line obstruction. Larger rings, widely spaced and with the butt ring well up the rod, make a lot more sense. How large is large? Well, that too is a question of personal interpretation. You are unlikely to find much benefit in a butt ring over 50 mm diameter. Selecting the rest of the set is a matter of progressively grading down the intermediates to produce a neat funnel for flowing line.

Hybrid multiplier/fixed spool ringing. Whip a 40 mm or 50 mm butt ring to Zone B so that there is at least 33 inches between the reel seat and the ring itself. (On most 11·5 foot blanks with the reel seat set at 30–32 inches you can usually afford a 36–39 inch gap). Glue on a 16 mm tip ring. Now space in 12, 16, 20, 25 and 30 mm intermediate rings so that the holes in the rings align into a

Daiwa's Dynaflo stainless steel insert ring.

conical tunnel as you look through the butt ring. The rod will handle both fixed spool and multiplier reels with no flow problems at all up to 200 yards. Load of casting and fishing is neatly absorbed by the entire working length of the rod. Turn the rod upside down—multiplier style—and you will find that line hardly touches the blank under full compression. Even on flexible tips which do exaggerate line drop, contact is of no consequence.

Fuji BSHG and Dynaflo rings are excellent. The butt ring may be a BSHG or the slightly lower BNHG depending on the height of the fixed spool face. A butt BNHG mixes nicely with a set of BSHG fitted higher on the rod—many custom builders think it looks neater than a complete set of BSHGs. Seymo rings are not quite high enough, nor are they yet available in large sizes. When these limitations are resolved this British ring will make its mark in surf fishing. The quality of the ring and the frame's elasticity ensure popularity.

Surf and casting rings in general. Choice lies between plain wire rings, aluminium oxide inserts, silicon carbide and hardened stainless steel in a cushioned frame. Each ring has its uses, though plain wire has little future.

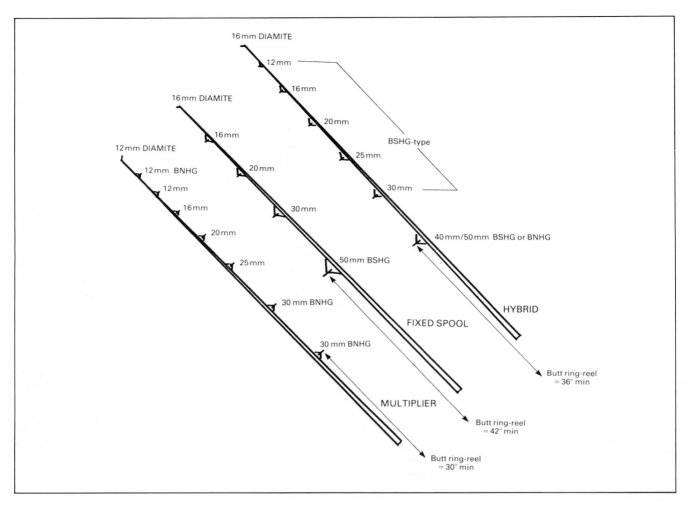

16mm DIAMITE
12mm
16mm
20mm
25mm
30mm

BSHG-type

16mm DIAMITE
16mm
20mm
30mm

40mm/50mm BSHG or BNHG

12mm DIAMITE
12mm BNHG
12mm
16mm
20mm
25mm

50mm BSHG

30mm BNHG

HYBRID

FIXED SPOOL

30mm BNHG

Butt ring-reel
= 36" min

MULTIPLIER

Butt ring-reel
= 42" min

Butt ring-reel
= 30" min

Plain stainless steel and hardchromed steel rings with soldered or spot welded frames offer good performance at low cost. Friction is minimal during the cast but somewhat higher under load, when there is always a chance of line abrasion and burning. Poor quality wire rings fitted to low-key Oriental rods often conceal wisps of loose chrome or patches of rust which cut stretched nylon.

High-quality wire rings, such as the Hopkins and Holloway series, have none of those drawbacks. Their only fault which is endemic in wire rings of all kinds, is fragility. It takes only a knock against the beach to distort a wire ring which will never rebend to perfect shape. Like other travelling anglers I have arrived on the beach to find my rod rings crumpled. Though I like wire rings for casting, I cannot reconcile myself to the risk of lost fishing. I no longer use them on my better fishing rods, though they are useful in testing blanks. They weigh so little that the full power and action of the rod are never masked which is sometimes the case with heavy lined rings.

The Fuji series of lined rings and other brands of the same design are much tougher than wire. You can be fairly sure that the ring will not be crushed beyond value on its way to the surf. There are other snags however: aluminium oxide centres pop out of the plastic cushion rings. Maybe that is no major disaster on a butt or intermediate ring, but if the tip ring bursts, then you are in trouble. The sharp metal frame cuts the leader in mid cast; or even if you are lucky enough to land the cast successfully, the edge of the ring carves out chunks of main line as you wind in. On the whole though, BNHG and BSHG rings are fine for all kinds of surf and distance casting.

Daiwa's Dynaflo rings are a valuable addition to the range of surf and long-distance accessories. The frame is strong and very similar to Fuji. Instead of an aluminium oxide centre, Daiwa use a hardened, low friction stainless steel insert. The inner cushion ring between frame and lining is almost hidden from view and therefore immune to popping. In this respect the Dynaflo is superior to most other rings, and a serious contender for top honours. Service life is the main reservation: Dynaflos lack the track record of other rings, simply because they have not been available for as long. Initial tests suggest they are as tough as necessary except for ultra-heavy fishing which tends to overstress the relatively high frame.

Whippings must be sealed for security. High-build resins are better than varnish. Rustin's Type F plastic coat is a good alternative to proper custom finishes.

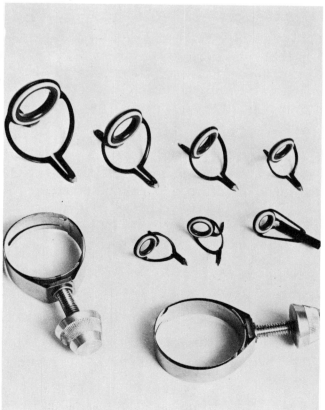

Fuji BNHG rings for multiplier casting.

Fuji offers a silicon carbide centered ring, which they claim cuts line friction and lengthens the cast. Like other surf casters who have tested the rings on a variety of blanks. I am unable to find any real distance advantage in Si C. They are nice to use, however, and are perhaps a little smoother under heavy retrieve pressure, which does highlight the friction coefficient of any material. The rings seems a bit stronger and more reliable too. Decide for yourself if the high cost is justified.

Hopkins and Holloway's Seymo ring for light surfcasting and spinning is the first decent British product for ten years. The frame with two legs moves freely with the blank but still supports the ring under pressure. Ceramic lining fuses to the metal frame without a cushion-ring. In all it is a neat design, worthy of the finest surf blanks. The present model is too low and too small for serious fixed spool casting, but larger versions are in the pipeline. The cost is highly competitive, which is a pleasant change with the price of other brands rising towards sheer blackmail.

Tip rings take a beating from casting, line retrieve and continual bashings on the beach. I am fed up with lined rings that pop open, tungsten carbide which shatters and narrow-edged centres that ruin leader and main line. All my best rods sport Hopkins and Holloway Diamite tips, which are solid almost indestructbile and great value for money. They are the only tip ring that I would care to recommend to keen surf men who cannot afford to make a mistake.

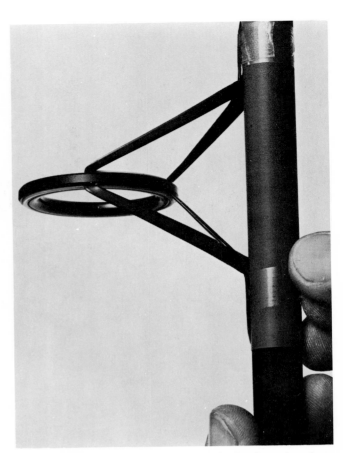

Fuji BSHG rings stand high off the blank for fixed spool work.

Friction—how can you reduce it?
I have read a lot of technical explanations by ring makers who almost wooed me into ripping apart my surf rods and rebuilding them with the latest Supercasting Rod Ring. Sceptical to the end, I restrain myself and borrow a set to test. I have never found one ring that cast significantly farther than another. There are rings that given half a chance would rip your line to bits. Others are as smooth as silk. None makes much difference to how far you cast, even under tournament conditions. In surf, with bait drag to contend with, you would not see a measurable improvement anyway, whatever the ring did. The microscopic gain in sinker energy due to lower line friction through the rings is far outweighed by the massive loss of distance from a single worm.

Lined rings, and silicon carbide in particular, are smoother under load, and more efficient than wire. You can feel the reduced friction; in this respect the makers are correct—low friction materials offer superior fishing. The mistake they make is to suppose that line flying through rings

Fixed spool attached to aluminium alloy butt by the Spanish method of wrapping with rubber strip cut from an inner tube.

52

Fuji FPS screw seat. An excellent choice for casting rods . . . but remember to keep the threads clean.

has significant pressure against the lining. It hardly touches, and that being so, varying coefficients of friction make no real difference. It is pressure of line on the edge of the ring, not the area of ring and line that touch, which most determines frictional losses. Maybe there is a difference between ring linings and in the lightest of freshwater fishing, where even the surface tension of water trapped in rings holds back the cast. Casting in the surf is never so complicated and no tournament was ever won nor record set because the caster had access to a magic ring. Size of rings, their position and spacing do make a difference. If rings choke the line, or spacing reduces efficiency of blank, corrective measures produce remarkable increases in performance and control. Those are points to consider when you design and build your own pendulum rod.

HANDLES AND ACCESSORIES

Hand grips. Powerful casting, pendulum or any othe good style, depends on a secure rod grip and correct distance between hands for leverage and speed. The simplest butt construction, still favoured by anglers who value utilitarian rather than decorative surf rods, is a plain handle of glassfibre, aluminium alloy or carbonfibre, either covered with shrink tube or left bare, and fitted with a pair of hosepipe clips which secure the reel. Sometimes there are no handgrips at all. Mostly,

for comfort and nonslip handling under pressure, the butt is wrapped with cord, tape, cork strips, plastic foam or leather built up to form separate grips at the butt cap and on both sides of the reel.

The plain parallel butt, lacking even simple handgrips, has the tremendous advantage of flexible reel positioning. Too many mass produced and custom built rods have the reel seat too high or low for precise casting. Even where the spacing is correct for one particular sinker weight, it is just too short or too generous for heavier and lighter tackle. For most surf anglers it really makes little difference. Expert casters searching for those extra few yards must have a reel that clips in exactly the right spots for 4, 5, and 6 ounce sinkers or whatever else they have to cast. They are happy to make do with a 'barebones' look to the rod in return for that range of adjustment.

For general fishing though, you can incorporate variable hand spacing by arranging permanent grips and reel seat so that the lower hand—the left for most casters—works on a grip about three inches longer than strictly necessary. If spacing for 4, 5 and 6 ounce casting is 29, 30 and 32 inches respectively from the centre of the reel seat to the end of the butt grip, you can make the butt 32 inches long, then hold the grip up to 3 inches shorter for the lighter weights. Set up the reel seat to cast the heaviest weight, then choose a butt grip length that matches any smaller sinker you intend to fish on that rod.

53

On most average length pendulum rods matched to 4–6 ounces of lead, a reel seat some 32 inches from the butt cap to the centre of the reel is perfect. Be wary of rods with substantially longer butts. Almost certainly they will not respond to the pendulum cast.

Most modern surf rods use three separate grips: the top pair about six inches long, the butt between 6 and 9 inches. Soft Neoprene, Hypalon and cork are excellent. Hypalon is perhaps the best, but must have walls less than ¼ inch thick. Too thick a wall sponges up hand pressure and wastes much of the casting energy. Aim for a comfortable grip with plenty of security and sensitivity. Watch the diameter as well because much over 1·25 inches across a grip prevents your thumb clamping down on the multiplier spool. The consequences of reel slip at full power are disastrous. If necessary prune the Hypalon with a sharp knife until the grip diameter no longer interferes with reel control. Strip it off altogether if you like, and replace with a strip of cork tape or thin-walled rubber. Tennis racquet handle and bike handlebar grips can be pressed into service if appearances do not worry you.

Reel seats. A pair of stainless steel hoseclips is adequate security for multiplier reels attached to parallel butts without grips. Elsewhere, a Fuji snap-lock clip or conventional screw seat is permanently fitted between the upper pair of handgrips. The snap-lock is bad news in my opinion—forever falling apart, and working efficiently in the first place only if the reel slots perfectly into the base. Many reels are too short for one serrated point on the retaining clip, too long for the next. The reel either slips around in the fitting or strains the mechanism. The device tends to rip apart under pressure anyway—usually when you hook a big fish. However, for all its failings, the snap-lock is suitable for lightweight surf and freshwater rods. Check that your reel fits the seat before building the rod. You will not be the first angler to spend days custom-building a rod to discover, after the glue has set, that your reel is incompatible with the chosen Fuji.

Of the screw fittings available, only Fuji FPS and others of similar materials and construction make sense for casting rods. Once a tubular seat is fixed with adhesive, it is there for life. Even if you cut the seat off in chunks, the rod butt has to be stripped before you can slide on a replacement. Metal seats are either heavy and overpowered for surf fishing, or of lightweight, corrodable aluminium alloy. Stick to stainless steel/carbonfibre Fuji-type for long service life and security. Seats require little maintenance other than washing and an occasional application of graphite powder or silicon spray to the threads. The screw seat also accommodates fixed spool reels comfortably, which is far from the case with snap-locks and hose clips.

Casters in Spain have evolved a neat and cheap fitting for fixed spool reels: they scavenge an old inner tube, which is cut into one inch strips, 18 inches long. These are bound tightly around the rod butt and reel stand to form a waterproof, soft combination of handgrip and reel seat. The end of the strip is tucked under the penultimate coil to hold the whole thing together. Neatly applied, a rubber strip is better than any conventional reel seat and may be instantly shifted to suit hand spacing.

Butt caps. Never cast without a soft rubber cap over the rod butt end. During the final stage of a pendulum cast, the butt drives down towards your lower left ribcage. Should the sinker snap off, the butt stabs hard into chest or stomach. The need for protection is obvious. Never use the metal spear fitted to some surf rods as standard equipment. It is potentially lethal. Cut it off and glue on a rubber cap, which can be homemade or custommoulded as you wish. A big hollowed out cork is better than nothing.

Multiplier Reels

Multiplier reels—American anglers know them as conventionals and baitcasters—feed line from a revolving spool driven by gears during retrieve and are free-running in mid-cast. For many anglers the conventional reel is never more than a dream. They would love to use one, but are unable to live with continual backlashes and burned thumbs.

If angling were purely an exercise to catch fish, few anglers would bother to learn multiplier casting. The fixed spool is so much easier to master, casts almost as far and winds in line more quickly. But objectivity is not the only aspect to consider. Angling is a mixture of technique and pleasure, mechanics and wishful thinking, competition and relaxation. Reels may achieve the same end results, but they do not feel the same in action. Multipliers are smoother, better balanced to the rod, compact and, above all, precise. In the hands of an expert, the multiplier reel sings. Fixed spools churn like 19th century mangles.

Although most problems of multiplier control are based on faulty technique, the design of a casting reel is important. Many reels cast tolerably well, but only a handful excel in the surf. Freshwater casters should make an effort to pick the best baitcasting reel for their sport—tiny spools are subjected to enormous speeds and pressures. Does the reel you own or aim to buy measure up to the following?

THE ESSENTIAL FEATURES OF THE MULTIPLIER REEL

Strong, light spool

The spool accelerates from zero to over 40,000 revolutions a minute within one tenth of a second when you cast a 5 ounce sinker 200 yards. Even a modest one hundred yard cast spins the reel fast enough to highlight any imbalance and weakness of spool. Ideally, use the lightest spool available. Plastics are acceptable but aluminium alloy is better. Medium-quality reels have sectional alloy spools composed of spindle, flanges and central core, pressed or screwed together. The very best spools are of machine cut, single piece alloy precision bored for the stainless steel spindle. Spool run-out is less than 0·003 inches which prevents thin line trapping itself between spool rim and sideplate. Heavy brass/chrome spools for deep sea fishing are always unacceptable for serious beach casting.

Smallest practical spool capacity

Your reel should be the smallest size compatible with the kind of fishing you do. Every inch of excess line reduces performance and encourages backlash. Maintain the theme by fishing with the lightest line considered safe for the species you hunt. A surf reel designed for 300 yards of 14 lb test is much easier to tune and control than one able to accommodate 300 yards of 30 lb test. The lighter reel probably casts 50 per cent farther too.

ABU 9000C, a large capacity surf reel of high casting and fishing performance.

Excellent bearings

High-performance casting ferrets out poor bearings and destroys them. Floating ball-races are best for long casting and fishing, though they are not totally superior to plain bronze bushes. Much depends on how keen you are to tune the reel. Plain bushes need continual attention and lubrication if they are to stay in peak condition. Ballraces soak up and retain plenty of lubricant, so you can fish and cast for several days without servicing the reel. Both cast extremely well, but the ballrace is smoother under heavy retrieve pressure; on the other hand, plain bearings run more quietly. Highly tuned ballrace reels may scream thoughout the cast.

Tough, rigid frame

There is no substitute for quality in this department. Flimsy reel frames and seats twist under load, destroy alignment of bearings and spool, and overload the gears. Many reels fail to withstand even six months of rugged surf fishing before the frame rots to powder, distorts, or pops away from the reel stand. Screwed, chromed brass frames are excellent although old-fashioned; single-piece machined frames of aluminium alloy are rigid but likely to corrode. The best compromise is a screwed together frame with substantial crossbars as for example, on the Penn Magforce series. Sectional frames have the advantage of adjustment and easy component replacement.

Strong, high ratio gears

Compared to fixed spool reels, multipliers are slow to retrieve line from long distance. As line level falls towards the spool core, even high-speed gears work hard to keep up with a fish or to lift tackle away from the seabed. Gear ratio should be at least 4.25:1. However, the higher the gear ratio, the lower the mechanical advantage of retrieve. Gears may be overstressed if you crank against a heavy fish—smaller tournament reels strip their teeth. Weak spools burst and even explode through the sideplates of the reel. Stainless steel machine cut gears are indispensible for heavy-duty surf fishing. Make sure they are of tough steel—some of the cheaper Oriental steel is soft as cheese. Bronze is an excellent material which soaks up punishment and does not rust.

Be careful with small baitcasters fitted with powerhandles (extend winding handles that boost leverage). They are no faster in retrieve but do encourage direct winching rather than pumping. The result is strained or broken gears and spools. Use them for the comfort they provide, not for additional power.

Useful for light surf and all-round freshwater casting—the new magnetically controlled Daiwa baitcaster.

ABU 6500CT and modified Daiwa Millionaires are favourite tournament reels with a reasonable beach peformance. What you gain in distance you lose in strength and retrieve.

56

Powerful, precise drag system

The trend towards lighter tackle in the surf exaggerates deficiences in drag design and operation. When working 12 lb test at long range, you cannot afford a drag that overheats and either locks solid or fails to grip, or limits the range of adjustments necessary to handle a big fish. Star drags should feel smooth and even as you tighten down on the brake plates. Never buy a reel which runs from free-spool to total lock-up within a single turn of the wheel. It is sure to let you down. Surf fishermen looking for big channel bass, tope, cod or even sharks on light line must not compromise here. Some European and Japanese casting multipliers have notoriously weak drags which burn out on the first big fish that rips 100 yards from the spool. Make sure the reel you choose has the right service back-up: you might need new drag washers every six months if you fish hard and hook lots of heavyweight fighters.

Casting controls

A well designed surf multiplier requires little spool control if correctly loaded and well cast. However, even expert casters rely on centrifugal or magnetic cast controllers to smooth out minor errors and to facilitate reel tuning. The older Penn reels cast extremely well without brakes if you use a plastic spool and thick oil in the bearings. Modern reels with aluminium alloy spools still respond to lubricant control but are better suited to a magnet or brake blocks. Beginners are most at risk unless their reels can be detuned for firm control. Even tournament casters appreciate the confidence inspired by a brake of some kind. It is not cheating to use a casting control . . . it is common sense to take the easy way out.

Corrosion resistance

Modern reels originally designed for freshwater fishing cannot really be expected to last long in the salt. However, even the purpose-built sea reels may fall apart in six months unless you flush out sand and seawater every trip. Aluminium sideplates and spools suffer terribly—usually the inside faces rot to powder. Plastic side plates and well anodised saltwater-grade aluminium frames ward off damage far better than lacquered alloy and cheap stainless steel. Take care to buy a good brand of reel, and be sure to look after it. That means regular maintenance, not a once a year springclean.

THE RIGHT REEL FOR YOU

There are casting reels you fish with, and fishing reels that cast. Choose according to how you fish

Any baitcaster or level-wind reel can be modified for better casting by cutting away the level-wind gears and crossbar. You must replace the front bar with a solid frame brace.

and what you hope to catch. Decide whether pure distance matters most, or if sacrificing 20 yards pays off in faster, rugged handling of big fish in turbulent seas and fast rivers.

Reels for sheer distance

High-performance reels—tournament and ultra-long range fishing—are very easy to tune and control, cast terrific distances in surf and freshwater and, with care, handle average fishing pressures. But at some stage you have to balance sheer power against peak casting performance. The reels listed here fall down, sometimes unacceptably so, when powerful retrieve, drag performance and operational speed are laid on the line. Maintenance is more critical—understandable since these models are plain or modified freshwater baitcasters. The most popular reels are:

ABU 6500CA
ABU 6500CAT
Daiwa Millionaire 6HM, 6HS, 6RM
DAM Champion 800B
Penn Levelmatic series

Their line capacity with level-wind mechanism removed averages 300 yards of 0·35 mm nylon monofilament or 250 yards of 0·40 mm. In standard form they hold about 15 per cent less. They all feature centrifugal brakes, tolerable gearing ratios and drags which range from barely acceptable to good. The Millionaires and the Levelmatics are strongest in this department. All reels

Laying on the first 50 yards of line is an important stage in reel tuning. Poor loading causes severe spool vibration.

except the Penn are wide open to saltwater invasion and subsequent corrosion. The Penn frame is the least desirable; Daiwa's single-piece frame is the best. DAM and Millionaire spools are single-piece machined aluminium while the others are sectional and not so tough. However, where casting distance counts heavily towards successful angling, all the reels are highly competitive and there is nothing much to choose between them.

Tough fishing reels

The next group of reels casts very well indeed but never equals the record breaking distances of baitcasters. However, they do offer tremendous bonuses for anglers who fish rough ground, heavy surf, for fast-running tope, stubborn channel bass and massive conger eels. The much higher rate of retrieve lifts tackle over weeds and rocks, whereas baitcasters wind sinker and hook straight to destruction. In real terms loss of range is comparitively marginal—under 10 per cent for the best anglers and of no consequence for the under-150s. Big reels are more difficult to tune, load and handle, however. On the other hand, they are built specifically for seafishing and are thus more resistant to

saltwater corrosion. Generally, drag systems are good enough, gears are tough and frames solid.

> ABU 7000, 8000C, 9000C, 10000C
> Penn Squidders and Surfmasters
> Newell 220F, 229F
> Penn Magpower 970, 980
> Mitchell 602AP, 600AP
> Policansky 2B

These reels suit all purses, capacity requirements and levels of sophistication. Some have ballraces, others plain bushes. Squidders and Surfmasters lack casting controls but are easily tuned with oil. ABU reels rely on centrifugal brake blocks, while the Penn Magpower series operate on a revolutionary new magnetic controller. Mitchells are cheap, serviceable reels. ABUs are nicely made but prone to corrosion unless thoroughly cleaned every trip. The frames are adequate, though not as good as Newell or Penn. Newell and Penn 970/980 reels are also very tough mechanically; the Penns are fitted with the Senator 4/0 offshore reel's big-game drag. You certainly cannot do much better than that.

Line capacity varies throughout the range, from 250 yards of 20 lb test on the Newell 220F to the ABU 10000C's 400 yard-plus. In the middle are reels which hold either 200 yards of 20–25 lb test for tough fishing on dirty ground and in heavy surf, or at least 350 yards of 0·40 mm diameter for everyday casting and fishing. Except for the big ABU, every reel on the list will cast close to 200 yards, given the right pair of hands. Shore fishermen can expect an easy 125 yards fishing range— behind the tournament reels perhaps, but still excellent. You see the benefits when a big fish runs hard or heads for rocks: these reels will stop him; the better-casting models may not. The lifespan of the bigger reels should be at least ten years, whereas many tournament reels are scrapped after two years' hard work in the surf.

Modified reels
Standard baitcasting multiplier reels are good enough for casting up to 150 yards or so but then the limitations of the level-wind system intrude on line flow, cut distance, and tend to trap the leader knot in the line guide. Most casters find that the top crossbar prevents a firm, deep thumb grip on the spool. It is now standard practice in the surf to cut off the top bar, remove the level wind bar and its internal gears, and to replace the level wind itself with a solid crossbar which strengthens the frame. Normally you do the work yourself or take the reel to a tackle shop or toolmaker with the necessary skills and machinery. Only ABU markets a production baitcaster without level wind, namely the Ambassadeur 6500CAT. A replacement CT cage is available (spare part Number 991) for existing 6500 series reels.

Removing the level wind also increases line capacity by around 25 per cent. That is why smaller reels cast over 250 yards despite having a quoted maximum capacity of less than 200 yards. Laying on line by hand also produces a neater, tighter load pattern which runs more freely and under better control. The reel also accepts a wider selection of line diameters since level winds usually work best with one or two diameters only.

Distance gains are in the region of 20 per cent with modified small baitcasters and less than 10 per cent on larger models like the ABU 7000. In fact, the 7000 gains so little from modification that very few anglers bother to remachine the cage. The only value is in preventing occasional snapped leaders due to knots catching in the line guide. Spool grip is the major consideration with all sizes of reel. If the spool slips under full power, it pays to get rid of the offending crossbar even if you are not interested in extra fishing range.

Other useful changes to standard production reels include replacement of spools and gears, frames and bearings with custom-made components that are faster running, stronger or less likely to distort under pressure of highly stressed monofilament. Newell specialise in modified parts for Penn reels, although with the introduction of the Penn aluminium alloy spools, higher gear ratios and better drag washers, the need is no longer significant. Newell frames are still an excellent investment if you have small hands and a short thumb. Extra reach created by low-set Newell replacement cages allows easier spool control and better distances.

Mass production tolerances are high enough to ensure your reel is satisfactory for general fishing, but might not guarantee the best possible performance. Check alignment of frame and spool. Make sure the spool is well balanced and evenly machined because you can have high and low spots which induce vibration at high speed. Check that bearings and gears are free from metal swarf and misplaced grease. If the reel will not run fast whatever you do, examine the right hand spindle and its drive sleeve which connects the spool to the gears. Often there is dirt, excess lubricant or too tight a fit between the components. Clean the drive train and if necessary polish it and the spindle. You may gain 20 yards.

Loading a multiplier
Rough running spools, poor distances and too many backlashes are symptoms of a badly loaded spool. Every inch of line on a multiplier is turning fast throughout every cast, regardless of distance. Poor line loading always results in vibration and loss of power. Light and heavy areas on the spool are magnified many times at high speed. Even the knot that attaches the bottom end of the nylon to the spool core must be correctly tied and positioned. A line level just ¼ inch too high makes some reels uncontrollable, while too low a filling slashes distances by 50 yards.

Tie line to the base of the spool with a timber hitch or blood knot. Tournament casters may tape the end with a tiny patch of Sellotape instead, but that is no good in the surf although it does help perfect spool performance. Just tie the smallest, neatest knot you can. I never bother to tuck it into the slot drilled into most spool centres; but there is no reason why one should not do this.

Wind line evenly onto the spool, cotton reel fashion, and under medium tension achieved by passing incoming line between finger and thumb. Load line until you reach the level that best suits your casting. Determine that by trial and erorr. To start with, fill baitcasters to within 1/16 inch of the flanges. Medium and large reels—Penn 970 and ABU 9000C for example—should be slightly underfilled by 1/8 and 1/2 inch respectively (with 0·40 mm line). The ABU is much easier to cast when deliberately kept low; but after practising for some time you will know the reel's characteristics well enough to raise the level if necessary. The rule with multipliers of all kinds is to err on the conservative side unless you have full capacity or can really control the beast.

Sometimes a reel fills unevenly for no obvious reason. Strip off the line and start again. Usually that does the trick. If not, try slightly thicker or thinner line, especially valuable on level-wind reels. Should everything fail, check the spool for accuracy. Some cheaper reels are inaccurate enough to destroy your best efforts, and the only answer is to change spools.

Reel tuning systems

Every well-designed beachcasting and freshwater multiplier reel is essentially docile provided that both rod action and casting style are compatible with the reel's operating characteristics. There are some pressures which defeat a multiplier no matter how well it is designed. And, provided you cast reasonably, the converse also is true—a well made reel is not particularly vicious or even sensitive to minor mistakes. Pendulum casters regularly get away with murder because the style itself compensates for a surprising level of incompetence.

Two stages of the cast most affect the multiplier: the initial surge of acceleration immediately after line release, followed by the free flow period onward of halfway through the cast. When you cannot control the multiplier, or want to check the degree of tuning, examine those two periods. Release phase backlashes occur within the first 50 yards, and more often inside 30 yards. Flow period problems begin between 75 and 100 yards out. Sometimes it pays to measure distances to confirm your suspicions.

In both cases you can tame the reel with brake blocks, magnets or even by squirting different viscosity oils into the bearings. Some direct control is always necessary to iron out the initial surge of acceleration and its immediate afermath, flywheeling, which is the tendancy for line flow to vastly outstrip sinker speed. BUT—and this is crucial to success—provided you use a well-designed surf reel, most overruns in release phase are due to bad technique. Nothing you do to the reel—short of overtightening bearing caps and inserting huge brake blocks—can possibly save the cast from a major backlash within the first half-second. If your casts fall into a pattern of RELEASE-SNAP, look to your technique. Provided the reel has at least two medium brake blocks, half-power magnet setting, or 140 grade oil in the bearings, backlash cannot really be due to anything except poor style.

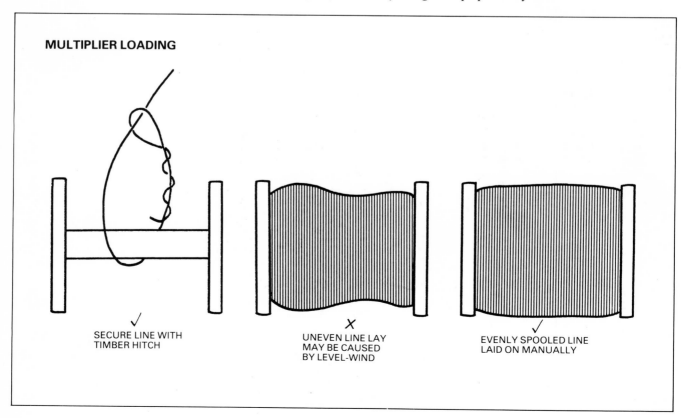

MULTIPLIER LOADING

SECURE LINE WITH TIMBER HITCH

UNEVEN LINE LAY MAY BE CAUSED BY LEVEL-WIND

EVENLY SPOOLED LINE LAID ON MANUALLY

Wind on line evenly and under moderate tension until the spool is moderately filled. Don't cram on every inch of line unless you know the reel runs controllably.

The leader knot could cut your thumb unless you tuck the end of the leader close to one side of the spool.

Adjusting the Penn 970's magnetic cast controller.

The other backlash pattern goes this way: RELEASE-SNAP and the cast gets away smoothly enough; the reel purrs into action, then fluffs up line and overruns. This classic rhythm signals either minor technique error or fractionally insufficient spool control. The sinker flies about 75 yards before the reel pushes off enough slack line to cause backlash. In both instances an increase of block size, a half-turn inward of magnet cap or upgrade in oil viscosity irons out the cast. No matter how well you cast, variations in wind speed, bait drag and sinker weight demand secondary tuning to ensure trouble-free fishing. Heat and cold also influence control settings. Expect any reel to speed up in summer and slow down quite considerably on a winter day.

Assuming your technique is pretty good, sinker, line and rod are balanced, and the reel is the right size and properly filled with light running line and strong leader, tuning is straightforward.

Centrifugal brakes

ABU and Daiwa Millionaires utilise two, three of four blocks according to model. I do not find it necessary to insert more than two blocks on any of them; missing blocks will not affect spool balance. Start with the biggest blocks supplied with the reel.

Adjust the bearing cap to allow a slight but definite end-float on the spool spindle, ignoring the recommended procedure of tightening the cap until sinker falls slowly from rod tip when the spool is released. Although satisfactory for some kinds of light baitcasting, this system of tuning is incompatible with long range pendulum work. The spool MUST float in the bearings.

Begin casting. Aim for nice, comfortable casts at first, then turn up the power. Backlash should be eliminated by the two big blocks. If not, work on your style, because that is where the fault lies. There is no point making the reel go any faster until snatch and ragged power flow are corrected.

Let us assume all goes to plan. Make a note of the maximum distances achieved. Now replace the blocks with two medium size ones. Repeat the casting exercise. Measure the distances and note the reel's response. Is it smooth and trouble-free, or does it fluff up a little in mid-cast? Again, there will be no definite overruns if you are casting well with at least 4 ounces of lead. Ligher sinkers, lures and plugs may cause problems.

Now go down to a pair of small blocks. Check the reel's reaction, and measure distances. Then, if you feel confident to carry on, take out one block. Run through the tests and make notes and measurements. For your last cast, take out the single block. At this stage you will learn one of three lessons: the reel overruns, which proves that

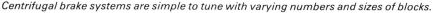

Centrifugal brake systems are simple to tune with varying numbers and sizes of blocks.

Not strictly necessary, but useful if the spool slips under your thumb—the Breakaway Thumbrake device fits all popular reels.

blocks really do work; the reel runs faster but stays under control and gives extra distance, in which case you must be casting extremely well; or the reel stays intact but does not speed up; a sign that something in the reel must be sticking: tight pinion or stale oil, perhaps. However, taking out of the last block is really an academic exercise. Normal results of brake block tests look something like this:

Block settings	Distance	Reaction
2 large blocks	105 yards	No backlash. Reel 'dead'.
2 medium blocks	115 yards	No backlash. Feels faster.
2 small blocks	130 yards	No backlash. Reel 'lively'.
1 small block	140 yards	Occasional backlash.
No blocks	145 yards	Backlash 3 casts out of 4.

The best setting here is 2 small blocks for routine fishing, or one block when the extra 10 yards are important. Weigh chances of backlash against better performance, then decide if the risk is justified. In the long term, work on your style so that single block casting is equally safe. This example is for smaller ABU 6500-type reels. Bigger models normally work safely and well with a pair of medium blocks, two small blocks or one medium. Much depends on tackle weight and line test.

Magnetic brakes

Test the reel in the same way, but this time work from full magnet power to minimum. Chart reel reaction, incidence of backlash and distances. You will soon arrive at the right setting. Remember to set the spindle end-float before starting to cast. Magnets are so easy to set up and so reliable that you may even be able to cast a couple of times then dial in the perfect setting. Apart from being a better control system than centrifugal blocks, magnets also provide stepless settings. Sometimes on other reels one block combination is a fraction too heavy, the next smaller a tiny bit too fast for comfort.

Oil viscosity

Old-style Penn and other simple reels have neither blocks nor magnets to monitor the cast, so, fill the bearings with 90 grade axle oil and make some test casts. If the reel is too fast, grade up to 140 oil or STP additive. If the reel is sluggish, use 20/50 engine oil. Most reels of Surfmaster 100 size loaded with 0·40 mm cast safely with 90 oil. Larger Squidders may require sticky STP. Try to maintain some end float on the spindle since the bearings and the spool will be ruined by overtightening, although a few, like the Mitchells, have special pressure pads which allow a certain amount of safe spindle tension. Traditionalists know that plain multipliers may be controlled by direct thumbing, however, handling a fast reel is quite an art. If all else fails, deliberately underload the reel, beginning with just 150 yards on Surfmaster 100s and 200 yards on the Squidder 140.

Fixed Spool Reels

The fixed spool reel (spinning reel) throws line from a spool set at 90 degrees to the handle axis. Nylon peels unhindered over the spool rim throughout the cast. Backlashes in the conventional sense are impossible. Tournament record casts are within 10 per cent of those set by the multipliers. In principle the reel is very efficient and easy to handle; but despite the potential advantages of fixed spools over multiplier reels, experienced beach fishermen generally still prefer the latter for sheer quality of sport.

On the fixed spool reel, the arrangement of gears and drive mechanism, plus friction from the bale arm roller which guides line onto the spool, add up to a rather unbalanced, clumsy reel. The mechanical efficiency never equals that of a multiplier, where the drive train is direct. Under full load, the fixed spool is an arm-aching beast with gear teeth, bearings and drive shaft subjected to immense pressure and consequently, only the finest reels are worth the investment for heavy-duty surfcasting.

Various sizes of reel cover all kinds of long-range work from ultra-light freshwater spinning to 8 ounce surfcasting. Despite the second-rate 'feel' and their limited winching power, fixed spools do come into their own in certain areas. Which reel should a long distance caster use—fixed spool or multiplier? For total flexibility he needs both. Their individual qualities complement each other.

The fixed spool's strengths

Fishing speed is perhaps the single factor that justifies using a fixed spool reel for long range fishing. Every multiplier, regardless of its gear ratio, is slow to retrieve from long distances. When the spool is even half empty, recovered line per handle revolution falls to a snail's pace. Gear ratio is irrelevant in this situation. A fixed spool reel fishes line quickly regardless of distance because spool working diameter is substantial, even with 200 yards of line out to sea.

Losing contact with hooked fish is common in long range fishing, and doubly embarassing when a fish runs towards you, throwing out yards of slack nylon which you cannot recover. More fish are lost through slack line than for any other reason. In big-money fishing matches, nobody is prepared to miss even one fish—it could just be the winning catch, worth thousands of pounds.

Many matchmen now use fixed spools to be sure that their lines do stay tight. The stronger reels are capable of withstanding fairly hard pressure, so there is no real danger of blowing up the gears by cranking quickly against slack line. Once in contact, you reduce winding speed anyway—full steam ahead with a big surf reel pulls the hook out of lightly pricked fish.

European beaches are overcrowded with anglers casting and losing miles of line, tons of leads and forests of terminal rigs. The more popular beaches—even of originally clean sand—are littered with a spider's web of semi-exposed monofilament and hooks. Slowly retrieved tackle tumbles across the seabed and sticks fast, adding to the mess. The only solution is fast retrieve to lift sinker and rig to mid-water where they plane back unobstructed. Fixed spool reels are ten times more efficient here and many beaches just cannot be fished without them.

Casting into the wind holds no fears for the fixed spool angler. No need to retune the reel, thumb the spool or reduce power. Hit the cast as hard as you like because the reel cannot backlash. (Wind knots are another matter but soon corrected). The only precaution is to avoid a massive belly of loose line which drifts into the tide or catches on a breakwater. High-speed retrieve comes to your aid once more: you can whip back the slack line while it is still hanging in mid-air.

Wind is often associated with cold weather. Together they are a nightmare for multiplier casters. Your thumb is sometimes so cold that it cannot grip the spool and the cast skids of control. Even if it does get away cleanly, wind pressure lifts the flowing coils and backlashes them. Controlling a hooked fish or merely retreiving tackle to rebait is sometimes impossible—your frozen fingers cannot grip the handle and will not guide line back on to the spool. A fixed spool takes the very worst weather in its stride.

Light line fishing is quite possible with a multiplier reel but generally easier with a fixed spool. Fixed spools grow more efficient as line diameter falls and thereby reduces spool rim friction. Multipliers do not show quite the same gains, at least not unless you reduce the size of reel as well, which in practical fishing terms may be impossible due to limited line capacity, slower retrieve and

The rear-set brake screw fitted to the Shakespeare Sigma reels and the ABU Cardinals is faster and more precise than the normal spool adjuster.

mechanical weakness. Even a big fixed spool can be usefully loaded with 10 lb test—and will, anyway, cast better than a smaller one. High sinker velocity creates tuning hazards for multiplier casters. Apart from leader knot flow and line twist, there is nothing to go wrong.

Learning to cast a fixed spool reel is much easier. But it is an advantage that might easily backfire. You can screw a fixed spool reel to a surf rod and cast without backlashes even if you have never been on a surfbeach before. Good news for the beginner, of course, but no blessing for the future.

The reel tolerates poor technique and even encourages it. Many casters brought up on the fixed spool can never change to multipliers because their ingrained casting technique is pitted with mistakes. It is far more difficult to break bad habits than to avoid them in the first place. Ideally, learn on the multiplier, then switch to fixed spool. Casting practice might be more painful for you in the first few weeks, but a good cast from a multiplier at least confirms that your technique is developing in the right direction.

THE RIGHT FIXED SPOOL REEL FOR YOU

PENN Spinfisher 750SS and 850SS
DAM 5001
MITCHELL 486 and 498
SHAKESPEARE SIGMA 080
SAGARRA TARZAN
ALCEDO

The reels here are all highly respected in surfcasting circles, all share good engineering standards—tough gears and drive shafts, corrosion resistant frames and strong spools. Individually, there are some differences mainly reflected in price. Mitchells are functional rather than sophisticated. What they lack in service life is made up with cheap spares and perhaps the best after-sales service of all. Penn fixed spools share the quality of the Company's multiplier reels; the drag is especially smooth provided you look after it. For overall engineering excellence, the DAM takes some beating—is exceptionally smooth under load and shrugs off corrosion except to the anodised spool.

The Shakespeare Sigma is without doubt the best of the Oriental fixed spools, and is fast, strong and saltwater-resistant. The rear-set drag screw complements the smooth and progressive brake plates, which are not located in the spool itself. In its way it is as unique as the Alcedo and Sagarra reels: both European, both rather dated in appearance—the Sagarra is plain ugly—but well made and offering high casting performance. The Alcedo—something of a collector's item (I wish I had one)—can be tuned for perfect line flow with the monofilament diameter you prefer. It's only obvious disadvantage is massive weight, but that is the premium you pay for substantial amounts of stainless steel. Almost every surfcaster in Spain, the Mecca of fixed spool casting, owns a Sagarra for fishing and tournament casting.

In contrast with the range of multipliers, this selection of reels does not benefit by individual comparison of casting ability and control. They are virtually identical, and of course none has, or requires, an anti-backlash controller. Pick the reel you like; within reason it will cast and handle fish as well as any other model. Real differences concern price which reflects, among other things, engineering standards, materials specifications and service life. The more you pay, the longer the reel will last. Does it matter, bearing in mind that all should give a minimum of three years hard work? That is for you to judge.

Every reel holds a massive amount of 0·35–0·40 mm line. Total capacity is irrelevant to casting. What counts is how the reel handles the top 250–300 yards, the maximum length likely to be drawn off the reel during a cast. Here there are no fears: listed models cast off that much line without generating excessive friction.

Spool format

Tournament casters argue the value of a large diameter, short spool against that of a narrower but longer line store. Differences arise in unrestricted tournament events where line breaking strain is way below 6 lb test, and spools are loaded into the perfect cone profile theoretically best for long distance casting. A long spool is better, mainly because it is easier to load into a cone. However, in beach and freshwater casting, and even for tournament work with lines around 0·35 mm diameter, the emphasis is better placed on diameter.

Popular saltwater reels are around 3 inches in diameter on the front. (2·75 inches–3·25 inches is the accepted range for top results). The average spool length—0·75 inches—means that 250–300 yards of 0·35 mm nylon take up no more than a 0·5 inch spool depth; if the spool is deliberately overloaded, even 300 yards stripped off still leaves a line level high enough to prevent excessive rim friction.

Minimal spool length brings design advantages in the gear train. The reciprocating mechanism has a short travel and is thus stronger and less likely to distort line profile. The spool can afford to move slowly backwards and forwards to produce a close-set line load. In contrast, the long spool strains gears and encourages ragged line lay. Spools for tournament casting have double bales which separately load the front and back of the coned spool. That is clearly impractical in the surf, and besides, usually does not operate smoothly with lines over 8 lb test.

All standard production reels are improved by modifications to the line profile and bale arm. The line level here is uneven, which reduces effective spool capacity by 150 yards.

Gear ratios

If anything, reels are too fast. Even a 3.5:1 gear ratio working through a 3 inch spool pulls back some 30 inches of line per handle revolution, which far outstrips a multiplier reel, and is sometimes too vicious on a lightly-hooked fish. Coupled to the relatively weak gear structure of the reel, a high gear ratio further reduces mechanical efficiency and promotes rapid wear in components of less than perfect quality. Look for machine-cut gears, not die-castings. Toughened stainless steel and bronze gears and shafts, ball-races and sturdy supporting frame are essentials in fixed spool design. Watch those points rather than worry about the precise gear ratio. Not that you have much choice: except for the special low-speed DAM reels, all fixed spools are geared more or less the same.

Drag systems

Fixed spool drag systems range from primitive to excellent. I am not surprised to see that European-made reels are generally poor, while those aimed at the American market offer more control, power and reliability. A typical European reel—Sagarra or saltwater Mitchell—is either free running or locked. There is not much scope in the mid-range pressure settings, and a strong likelihood of severe juddering or seizure under full load. The DAM is an exception. On the other hand, European anglers do not hook fish that make long, searing runs. Mostly they never give the fish an inch of line.

Reels popular in America and other game-fishing countries rely on good drag systems with powerful but progressive braking, burn-resistant plates and washers, and built-in anti-lock devices. Penns and Shakespeare reels are quite good in this respect; in fact most reasonable quality American and Oriental reels are satisfactory.

The drag mechanism has two purposes in long-range fishing; unfortunately they are antagonistic. You need a fighting clutch with a wide power band and strong resistance to locking up. Hard casting is impossible without a totally locked spool.

Reels with poor drags are usually easily locked for casting, but you suffer if you hook a big fish. The super-quality game drags either will not lock the spool at all, which is exactly the designer's intention, or by so doing they strain screw threads to stripping point. Overtightening destroys a good drag anyway. Once locked, reels like the Penns and Shakespeares never do revert to their previous smoothness and control. In fact, destruction of balance by deliberate overtightening seems a feature of the very best reels.

This is something you will have to come to terms with, either by intentionally ruining a fine brake system or by investing in a reel which does lock without too much trouble. The only alternative is a special modification to the spool skirt as described later, but even that is rough and ready. What anglers really need is a fixed spool reel with a separate locking device. It need not be part of the main drag.

Reel stand security

My general misgivings about Oriental reels centres on weakness of construction rather than on design itself. I cannot come to terms with gears that strip or crumble, bale arms that corrode, or shoddy finish. Most of all, I hate reels that snap off at the reel stand in mid-cast. Cheap castings of low-grade aluminium alloy cannot stand up to a big pendulum cast. There is no way to predict strength and life of a reel stand. Invest in a good make of fixed spool. Should the worst happen, at least you have a reasonable chance of replacement under warranty. Rotor housings seem to share the same fate as the stand; again, cheap castings are the culprit.

Spare spools

Spare spools are neither provided with some reels nor available separately. This is a sad reflection on some manufacturers who presumably do not realise that fishermen mess up their lines and need to change nylon diameters to compensate for varying casting weights and weather conditions. One spool seriously limits the scope of any fixed spool reel, saltwater or fresh, and cannot be tolerated by keen casters. You should ask about spares before you buy the reel.

LINE LOADING AND PROFILING

No fixed spool reel casts efficiently unless fully topped up with line. The level must be no more than 0·125 inches below the spool rim, and ought really to be well up on that figure. The majority of tournament casters and long range beach fishermen deliberately cram on every last yard of line the spool can accept without binding in the rotor head and bale. Top casters start with a 'normally' loaded spool, then wind on the extra 200 yards or more required to produce those massive distances.

Absolute capacity is not necessary for routine fishing. Too much line is fine for tournaments which involve perhaps ten casts all day, after which nylon is stripped off and replaced. A single day's fishing twists line and destroys the original perfect spool profile. Line sloughs off in clumps—either drips off the spool at random or rips off in mid-cast, sometimes taking a few rod rings with it.

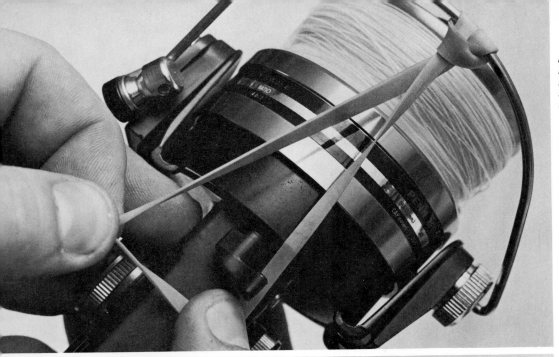

If you don't want to cut off the bale arm wire, loop a rubber band between the open bale and the gear case. The reel will cast without snapping shut.

Bale arm removal is simple— usually a matter of cutting off the wire with a handsaw. Even if the reel snaps over during the cast, line will not trap itself.

Re-profiling the lower section of line for better spool control and frictionless casting.

The re-profiled spool filled to capacity. The slight positive cone effect isn't necessary for beachcasting though may add a few yards in tournaments.

Lay the leader knot snugly against the back edge of the spool—it's less likely to foul during the cast.

Remember to lock the spool before casting hard with a powerful surf outfit. Line slipping against a bare finger will cut to the bone.

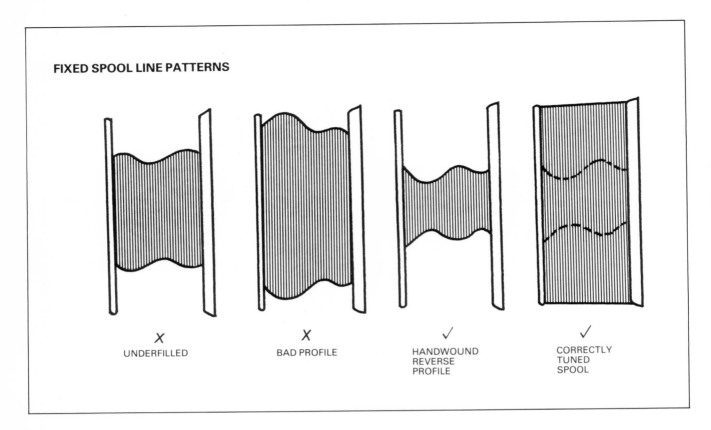

FIXED SPOOL LINE PATTERNS

X
UNDERFILLED

X
BAD PROFILE

✓
HANDWOUND
REVERSE
PROFILE

✓
CORRECTLY
TUNED
SPOOL

Level loading or perhaps a slight excess is acceptable. As always, avoid underloading the spool—that is where you lose most of your casting power.

Anglers are puzzled about the even line build up on a tournament caster's fixed spool. When they fill their own, line builds up excessively high or low—usually at the back or front face of the spool. Any reel chosen at random from the tackle shop shelf has this nasty habit. So how do leading fishermen produce such neat results? Are reels handpicked, the cream of the manufacturer's stock? Are they custom-made? No, they are simply profiled—a ten minute modification you can do at home without spending any money. You can be sure of casting farther, wasting less line and preventing all but occasional tangles.

Load your reel to the brim with line. See where high and low spots occur. Make a rough sketch of this line profile, then strip off around 275 yards of line. Refer to the sketch. Now, wind on line by hand or by spinning the spool in a lathe. DO NOT use the normal winding mechanism, because this time you are aiming for a profile which reverses the normal pattern of humps and hollows. Using around 50 yards of handwound line, produce a REVERSE profile deep in the spool. The diagrams show you how the system works. Then top up the spool normally. The lower profile cancels out the reel's natural line lay pattern, and should produce an evenly loaded spool with a flat profile or a slight positive cone. You may need to re-run

the experiment a few times to develop perfect lower profile, which is different for every reel. Even reels of the same model throw slightly different profiles.

You will also discover that because the reel now capitalises on the full spool volume, line capacity is raised by about 10 per cent. When you stripped off 275 yards, you will need 300 to replace it. Changing lines is easy: strip off the old line down to the re-profiled, handwound section, then top up the spool lip. Most casters use the lower profile as a permanent arbour. Layers of tape wrapped around the shaped core maintain correct profile and spool capacity.

Re-profiling eliminates humps and hollows and reduces, but seldom corrects, a reel's normal bias toward the back or front of the spool. In minor cases no correction is necessary. Reverse coning—too much line in front—exaggerates tangles, cuts distances and reduces spool capacity.

Either build up or reduce the thickness of the spool base washers, which moves the spool back or forwards relative to the line roller, or rework the bale arm mechanism with shims, (or by filing away the support posts), until the roller angle throws line further forwards or backwards. Some ingenuity and kitchen table surgery are required, since only the DAM 5000 series and Alcedo have adjustable components. The DAM drag/spool support plates is specially slotted for instant cone correction. The Alcedo is more versatile—even the bale arm moves for precise alignment. However, the process is simple enough on any reel, demanding only patience, plus a file, spare washer or two, and maybe a spot of epoxy filler.

BALE ARM MODIFICATION

Full bale arm mechanisms, designed to flip back into operation when the reel handle is rotated after casting, are a nuisance for long range casting and may well ruin your attempts to blast a sinker over 150 yards. The bale is so sensitive to rotor head momentum that it triggers prematurely, drops the roller back over the line in mid-cast and thus kills distance. In extreme cases line snaps. At worst—but surprisingly common on cheap reels—casting force rips the rotor head apart or even snaps the reel stand from the gear case.

Sagarra Tarzan, Mitchell 498 and Penn Spinfisher 706Z reels dispense with a full bale arm. Line is controlled by a roller on a fixed post. To cast, lift line from behind the roller. Afterwards, guide it back into the pick-up with your finger. Bale closure is eliminated; the chances of line fouling the roller during the cast are small enough to be discounted. Even for fishing lures on the surface, where the full bale arm is generally considered superior, the manual roller pick-up is quite adequate.

A home-made leather finger guard encourages better casting. Without fear of cuts and line burn, you'll be far more confident especially with the heavier sinkers.

DAM 5001 reels are tuned with an adjustable washer which raises and lowers the spool relative to the pick-up roller.

Experienced casters take a hacksaw to the bale wire and sever its connection top and bottom: close to the roller mechanism and tight against the opposite side of the rotor. Some reels anchor the far end of the bale wire with a bolt or screw set directly into the rotor. Most modern reels feature an external counterbalance weight which accepts the bale wire by screw or internal swaging. It does not matter how the wire is detached. More important is that you must replace the counterweight itself. Without extra mass on the rotor, the reel feels lumpy at speed, and eventually knocks outs its bearings.

The German DAM fixed spool reels are fitted with a variable bale arm spring device which raises or decreases bale arm trigger pressure. By resetting the internal tensions you can sometimes prevent bale flip without resorting to surgery. The alternative on other reels is to secure the bale open with a rubber band stretched tightly between bale wire and gear cage. It is a clumsy modification that works very well if you do not want to lose automatic bale action.

Reduction of spool rim friction

The majority of saltwater fixed spool reels are designed excessively broad, slightly too high spool rims. Distance is improved without loss of line control by lathe work—either polishing up or turning down the rim. Reels like the Sagarra Tarzan which have the same diameter rim front and back are much more efficent after being reworked to reduce the front diameter about 0·25 inches. Other reels are less of a problem and should not be cut down by more than 0·10 inches. Do not go mad on the lathe—reduce the diameter slightly, then test the reel. You cannot put metal back.

Spool lock modification

A crude but highly effective modification enables you to lock the spool for hard casts without straining drag plates or even altering brake setting. Only skirted spools respond to this treatment.

Watch how the spool reciprocates relative to the underlying rotor head. Pick a spot well forward on the spool, and drill a 0·25 inch hole through the alloy, so that the hole itself clears the rotor when the spool is fully advanced.

Cut a 2 inch piece of 16SWG or thicker stainless steel wire, and bend it into an even sided 'U' shape. Slightly splay out the last 0·125 inches of each leg to form a hook. Adjust the width of the 'U' until modest finger pressure compresses the clip enough to slide neatly into the spool hole. Release the clip, and it should grip tightly. Now connect the clip to the reel stand with a piece of 50–80 lb test monofilament.

Rotate the spool in the opposite direction to line-lay until the anchor line tightens between inserted clip and reel stand. Check that the spool is firmly restrained and that the anchor line itself neatly aligns with the spool, as the picture shows. Now pull back the bale arm or release line from the manual roller . . . cast as hard as you like. You will find the modification very easy to operate and absolutely reliable. The drag setting is never disturbed for casting; you will not strain plates or forget to reset pressure after each cast.

Casting releases

Supermen and gorillas do not cut their index fingers when casting a saltwater fixed spool reel at full power. The rest of us slice skin or at least rub it away through prolonged friction. A finger cut from an old leather glove secured by a piece of elasticated tape running around your wrist makes life far more comfortable. You will cast more confidently and consequently distances must improve. The leather shield—rubber is just as good—is far superior to various release gadgets on sale. Most are too imprecise at best; at worst they severely abrade line or snap the cast.

LINE TWIST

All fixed spool reels twist line. In theory, cast and retrieve counteract themselves. In practice they do not and eventually the line twists itself into knots. The only difference between reels is how long it takes to do the damage.

Load line as tightly as you can. Keep the tension high as you fish, which is easily achieved by running line between finger and thumb. Combing nylon this way also drives the majority of twists into the top 15 yards of main line, which can then be cut off. Ironing twists from an uncut line is not so simple. Try running off all the line, then drag it through surf or over long grass before respooling—time consuming and none too effective but better than nothing.

Lure fishing soon generates line twist and wind knots, which are aggrevated by soft, saturated nylon. Keep the line tight, and use brands of line which err towards the slightly stiff side when dry. The best line for fixed spool casting in conditions which exaggerate twist—lure fishing mainly—is DuPont's totally waterproof Prime cofilament. It is even better than Stren for preventing wind knots. One thing for sure is that swivels are downright useless for anti-twist fishing and anti-kink vanes are not much better.

SIDE-CASTERS

The Australian Alvey sidecasters are big, tough winches that swivel through right angles to cast fixed spool style. Various models cover the full saltwater and heavy freshwater range, and you can specify a star-drag system if you like.

Though not really suited to short rods with a high-set reel seat, the Alvey is at home on long surf rods cast South African and pendulum style. Distances and fishing control are excellent; the main headaches are sheer weight, poor balance and massive line twist. A valuable reel for rugged work, but unlikely to suit the majority of anglers.

The wire clip modification which anchors the spool without straining the drag system. Any skirted-spool reel may be altered.

Shock Leaders and Reel Lines

SHOCK LEADERS

A shock leader is a few feet of heavy nylon line tied to the main reel line to absorb casting stress. It provides some insurance against losing a big fish in breaking surf—a stage in the fight where you need all the help you can get. A strong shock leader also masks severe errors in casting style and timing: not an ideal property, but at least some protection for tackle and bystanders.

Good leaders certainly aid casting, if only because they permit the reel to carry light running line which would snap were it not shielded from initial shock and abrasion. In practical terms a leader allows long range fishing with 12–18 lb main line regardless of sinker weight. Plenty of line can be stored on a small reel, which is easy to handle and better casting than one which holds 250 yards of 30 lb test—the traditional line load.

Above all, shock leaders boost your confidence. No matter how hard you cast, the line remains intact during the power stroke. The generous safety margin protects terminal tackle and your neighbours on the beach. A leader is the guarantee that your tackle will not snap off and smash into somebody's face. On today's crowded beaches safety alone makes the routine use of shock leaders a moral obligation.

The more way-out casting styles are dangerous even with a shock piece, and you cannot be sure that tackle will hold together during peak power. Super-heavy nylon at least ensures a margin of safety. For most anglers who use ordinary pendulum techniques, though, the risk of skittering a sinker downbeach is considerably reduced by even 40 lb test leaders.

Unfortunately the confidence inspired by a shock leader can wreck your casting in the long term. To understand how, consider what heavy nylon does in mid-cast. *It is a shock absorber which irons out excessive tension between rod and sinker.*

In theory a leader is unecessary. When sinker follows rod correctly though the casting arc, very little strain develolps. You can calculate the forces involved: even on a 200 yard cast with 5 ounces of lead, the perfect style generates nowhere near enough leader tension to snap 40 lb nylon, a modest breaking strain by today's fishing and tournament standards.

Level line tournaments, in which line diameter must be constant from sinker to reel core, spring some surprises for casters who cannot cast without a leader. Four ounce sinkers really are cast over 200 yards on 18 lb line all through. Top competitors seldom snap off. Technique is the key—the cast flows like syrup with absolute smoothness of power. Every ounce of casting effort is precisely channelled into the blank and by sheer experience the caster knows just how near to breaking point he can stress the nylon.

Why not learn to dispense with a leader? Primarily because most casters—even good ones—easily overload normal surf fishing tackle and therefore risk snapping off every cast. Except for short range fishing, increasing line diameter and breaking strain to compensate for power input is not the answer. The thicker the line, the more distance is lost. By retaining the thinnest practical main line and shielding it with a leader, you reach a neat compromise. Even in top-flight tournament casting where styles are close to perfect, leaders boost performance by insulating the caster from the phsychological pressure of potential snap-offs.

Occasional casts inevitably lose control. Peculiar stresses develop when the sinker flies one way while the rod pulls another. Then follows a surge of excess pressure along the leader. The lighter the line, the less room for error. A strong leader mops up pressure and will probably save the cast unless the impact is particularly savage.

The cast either feels normal, or tightens and seems 'solid' and harsh—a sensation difficult to describe but instantly recognisable when accompanied by a burned thumb. The exact result depends on how bad the cast really was.

Real difficulties creep in when the leader disguises permanently bad style. Some men snap 50 lb leaders like cotton, yet they seldom cast more than 120 yards. Total lack of control is the problem here. They cast one way . . . the rod pulls in another plane . . . the sinker flies off just anywhere. Without fluidity of tackle and technique, it does not take much physical effort to snap strong

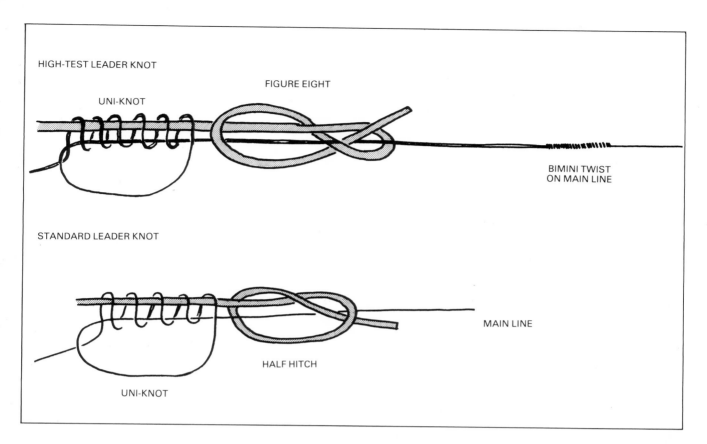

HIGH-TEST LEADER KNOT

FIGURE EIGHT

UNI-KNOT

BIMINI TWIST
ON MAIN LINE

STANDARD LEADER KNOT

MAIN LINE

HALF HITCH

UNI-KNOT

leader. Many fishermen suffer to some extent, and the fixed spool reel aggrevates the situation because it does not overrun in response to a bad cast. Bad casters murder their tackle, confident of avoiding backlash.

Obviously there are practical limits below which occasional snap-offs occur. There are rare casters who really can break heavy leaders even though they cast smoothly—some leading tournament competitors would never be happy with less than 50 lb nylon. But the modern trend towards very heavy leaders is detrimental to average fisherman.

Safe breaking strain depends on casting style, rod action and power, blank length and sinker weight. Extra poundage should be added to compensate for poor knots—we all tie them sometimes—line abrasion and deterioration within the line material itself.

As a rule of thumb, calculate safe leader breaking strain by multiplying sinker weight by ten, and calling the result pounds. Five ounce sinkers cast safely and easily on 50 lb test monofilament; 3 ounces requires a minimum of 30 lb test for absolute security.

Away from crowds, when beaches are deserted or long distances prove unecessary, I cut breaking strain to the lowest figure I know by experience to be manageable. For 125 yards fishing with 4 ounces and a fairly soft pendulum rod, I tie on 30 lb nylon, which never snaps in mid-cast. Run a few tests to establish realistic minimum line tests for the various rigs you cast. Choose a safe area to practise, and progressively reduce leader strength until you find the bottom limit.

Casting 4 ounces on 30 lb leader is a reasonable test of casting smoothness and efficiency. If you consistently break off under 150 yards, something is lacking in power flow or tackle balance. You should be able to reach the target in perfect safety with just 20 lb level line. Very good technicians do it on 15 lb monofilament.

Selecting and attaching leaders
Buy leader nylon in small quantities because some lines deteriorate rapidly. Were you to buy 1000 yards at once—anything up to 10 years supply—most would be seriously weakened or ultra-stiff by the time you half emptied the spool. Much depends on brand, material and how long it has sat on the dealer's shelf. As it is impossible to predetermine nylon's age and keeping qualities, it is wiser to opt for 50–250 yards at a time. That way you reduce losses should line fail on strength or pliability.

Many brands of nylon are naturally harsh and brittle. Others are pitted, crazed, nicked and of irregular diameter. All cast poorly and may snap without warning. On the other hand do not assume that all expensive lines are superior. Some cheap brands are excellent; but in general it does pay to invest a little more for DuPont Prime and

High quality line is essential for light-tackle surfcasting. It's no good wasting money on inferior monofilament and expecting miracles. Tackle-shy species like bass sometimes won't take baits presented on heavy traces—nobody can afford to take chances with cheap line.

Stren, Berkley Trilene, or even Maxima which though stretchy is still a good leader for general fishing. Of the cheaper brands, Sylcast is reasonable but very stiff in high breaking strain; Triple Fish and Ande are soft and tough. The very best leader? For my money it is Stren.

I am not sure if leader colour has any serious affect on fishing. I have caught fish on blue, green, brown, black, colourless, red and fluorscent gold. I would not rule out variations in catch rate even though there is no evidence to suggest that fish swim away from certain colours. I believe the opposite does occur—a few species are ATTRACTED by the leader. Surface-feeding schools of bluefish sometimes attack fluorescent gold Stren. European flatfish like daps and flounders, well known for their curiosity, bite well on Stren fluorescent blue or gold traces.

Too many anglers unroll a few feet of nylon and tie it to the main line without thinking about leader's correct length. Leaders cut for casting practice should give at least six full turns of heavy line on the spool when the sinker is suspended from the rod tip ready to cast. An extra 24 inches are worth having so that the leader can be retied several times before you lose the six anchoring coils.

Fishing leaders must be at least that long for safety, and might benefit from an extra ten feet so that you have some leeway for pulling a heavy fish through high surf. Never allow the knot to lie outside the rings when the fish beaches itself. One big swell followed by a powerful backwash sweeps the fish out to sea and snaps the main line at the leader knot. The rougher the water, the longer the leader should be.

However, too much leader ruins the cast. The knot MUST be off the reel and through the rings before the spool hits full speed, which is almost instantaneous after sinker release. If you use more than 50 feet of shock leader for really hard casting, expect the knot to wrap itself in the rings.

Cast clearance and line flow are dependent on small, streamlined knots between leader and reel line, but as plenty of fish are lost through weak knots, you cannot afford to compromise on knot strength. There is no alternative to a special leader knot similar to those illustrated. For everyday fishing and casting practice, the simple half-hitch/ Uni knot is fine. Serious light line work with heavyweight species demands the more complicated Bimini Hitch/Albright combination. Learn to tie both.

Sinker and trace attachment points are equally important, for they too present a safety hazard. If anything, the sinker knot is even more important than the upper joint between leader and main line. Sinkers snap off in mid cast because the knot was seriously weakened by seabed abrasion. There is no excuse for losing tackle this way. The angler who does so is a menace since all too often sinker, trace and hooks fly down the beach rather than seaward.

There is no substitute for a tough metal link between sinker loop and leader, or for a strong swivel or split ring between leader and trace. Mustad oval split rings are excellent—a direct replacement for swivels in most cases. Stainless steel wire clips work well too. Avoid flimsy link-swivels and safety-pin clips. The best swivels generally available are Berkley and Dexter. At all costs avoid cheap Oriental copies which pull apart under finger pressure, or rot to powder after a dousing of seawater. Someone's life may be at stake here. You cannot afford to take a risk.

Change the sinker/leader knot every dozen casts. Check every knot before each cast, and retie if you have the slightest doubt. Examine split rings and swivels too.

Leader softness

Above all you need a soft leader. Tough, wiry brands will not fly off the spool—fixed spool or multiplier—and they cannot snug down neatly when tied to reel line. Cheap nylon usually has a strong spool memory and springs back into coils when tension eases. The leader knot catches in the level wind or butt rings; main line tangles plague fully loaded fixed spool reels. Leader, trace and baits crumple into a mound of bunched nylon as

Stren, Trilene and Maxima are the best lines to consider for surf and long distance fishing. Stren (and the new Prime cofilament also from Du Pont) is outstanding even in this select trio of lines.

By using thinner lines, you can substantially boost the capacity of surfcasting reels. The ABU 6500CT holds over 300 yards of 0·35 mm (15 lb test) nylon.

soon as the sinker hits the water. You will also discover that springy, glossy brands of nylon tend to burn themselves and scorch your thumb as well.

MAIN LINE

Compared to the cost of rod and reel, transportation, bait and effort involved in learning to surfcast, the most expensive brands of line are dirt cheap. In real terms, expensive brands are usually more economical anyway because they last much longer. Some casters claim to change line every time they fish. The cheap brands they use are burned, abraded and cut after a single day on the beach. According to their logic, it pays to buy cheap line which you can afford to treat in cavalier fashion.

I do not see the sense in that way of thinking. The Stren and Prime lines that fill my reels are so tough and reliable that even 8 lb test lasts up to six months, unless of course, I snap off in mid-cast. One spool of 12 lb Stren has been cast over grass, fished from sand, rocks and shingle for a whole year. It is as close to perfect as you could wish. I

am free from continual nagging doubts that go hand in hand with cheap line: is this spoolful safe to use? Is the breaking strain accurate? Is there a weak section to give way when I hook a big fish? Extra money spent on good line is always repaid and it probably amounts to less than one per cent of your annual fishing costs anyway. Maxima and Trilene are useful alternatives to Du Pont line, although not quite so good for saltwater fishing.

Of the cheaper lines, Sylcast, Ande and Bayer Perlon (the soft version) seem fair value despite their limitations. Under no circumstances do they rival the high-grade lines—but they are good enough for learning to cast and for anglers who do not fish particularly hard or often. It makes no sense to load up with Trilene or Stren if you expect an overrun next cast. Lesser nylons encourage you to keep practising. Buy a bulk spool to begin your casting career, master your tackle, then upgrade to pure quality. Use the cheaper line once more when you test out a new rod or reel, or change casting styles. Most keen anglers have favourite 'ordinary' and 'best' brands of fishing line.

Breaking strains and diameters

Confusion still runs riot in casting line selection. Over the years, the largest selling breaking strains of nylon show a steady fall from 20 lb plus, to 18 lb, and now to 12–15 lb test. Information and confidence feed slowly into the angling world—for a long time anglers did not believe you could fish in saltwater with anything under 30 lb breaking strain. Modern tackle and techniques encourage a swing to lightness, but diehards still will not listen. The fact remains that you probably cannot utilise the full strength of even 10 lb line on a powerful surf rod and reel. 12–15 lb test nylon provides a good safety margin: with it you can land massive fish, even in rough water. If you still doubt the resilience of modern lines, tackle up with 15 lb line—even cheap stuff—and test it for yourself. Try to deliberately snap it.

Thinner lines cast farther, improve bite detection, reduce tidal pressure on sinker and rod tip, and provide enough stretch and bounce to cushion rod and line itself from sudden strain. Stretch and its associated spool crushing pressure impose certain restrictions on tackle and how it is used, but with modern reels there is no serious problem. Stretch is largely controlled by line quality. High-grade monofilaments and cofilaments are safe and

sensitive without being as rubbery as inferior lines, which can be a menace at long range.

Diameter/breaking strain ratios vary but have little effect on routine casting and fishing. Choose by diameter if you like, and leave breaking strain to look after itself. 0·35–0·40 mm is now the accepted specification for long-range beach fishing with tackle capable of handling heavy fish, rough water and big sinkers. Breaking strain falls between 12 and 22 lb according to brand. 15 lb is about average, and perfectly safe. What you gain with the 'strong' lines may be lost in handling qualities. Many are tough, wiry and susceptible to burns. Knots seem to cut themselves apart.

In specific conditions it pays to use heavier line throughout. Conger eel fishing and codding in rocky ground is short range sport which demands extra power to cope with obstructions and floating weeds. A 25–40 lb line on a large casting multiplier provides easy 100 yard fishing plus crane-like winching power. However, it takes a lot of muscle to achieve and maintain a 20 lb line pressure. Most of the extra power is illusory but the tackle is immune to abrasion and rough handling. Strong line helps winch a ten pound cod up a hundred yards of vertical cliff. Some anglers actually do use a crane fashioned from bicycle wheels.

Sinkers

A surfcasting sinker is a chunk of moulded lead which costs next to nothing compared to the outlay on rods and reels. Yet it is important because it helps control your casting and fishing techniques. Unless the sinker is matched to rod and reel, you are in big trouble during the cast and when the bait is in the water.

A sinker draws power from your muscles during the cast, then expends it to drag tackle and baits through the air. It can generate no more energy than you apply, so its efficiency as a projectile is directly related to your casting ability and strength, which are transferred to the sinker by the blank. Its length, action and stiffness must be carefully chosen—neither soft enough to waste your skill nor so overpowered that the blank cannot bend without brutal treatment.

The released sinker is a tremendous driving force. Mass and speed act together to pull the baits, terminal rig and line skyward. In so doing, the sinker must overcome gravity, air resistance and the mechanical drag of the reel.

Maximum speed of the sinker limits the kind of baits you can fish. The faster the cast, the more bait is torn from the hook. If flight speed is beyond the capacity of the reel, the spool is uncontrollably fast or hopelessly sluggish. Problems escalate with soft baits like crabs and mussels.

On the seabed, the sinker is either an anchor or a means of limiting tackle drift. It must be carefully matched to tidal current, size of bait, fishing range, depth of water and to line diameter. The sinker's resistance as it tumbles over the seabed on retrieve generates line tension. Because stressed nylon monofilament stretches up to a quarter of its original length, line wound back on to the spool imposes a crushing pressure measured in tons per square inch. Sinkers grossly mismatched to line, reel and rod can literally explode the spool and rip out side-plates.

A sinker's three major tasks—absorption of casting power; release of that energy in mid air; seabed control of the baits and terminal rig—must each be considered alone and in relation to the rest of the outfit, to the angler himself, to baits, fishing conditions and even to the expected species of fish.

The most useful sinker is one that offers the best solution in the circumstances. Sometimes it is impossible to choose one weight or shape which perfectly balances all the options. Often a compromise is essential. However, it must be thought out, not guessed at.

Sinker weight

Theorectically, you can cast far enough with any weight of lead. Power generated is related to sinker mass and velocity. The lighter the lead, the faster it flies. Big sinkers accelerate more slowly, but still develop comparable kinetic energy because of their higher mass. More important is momentum—'carrying power'—the product of mass and velocity.

Tournament casters achieve long distances with a variety of sinkers. One or two specific weights provide the highest performance under ideal conditions, but as a rule there is little to choose between 4, 5 and 6 ounce sinkers cast on appropriate diameter lines.

On the beach, the theory does not work out so well. Small sinkers simply cannot manage, particularly into a headwind. They have to fly so much faster to achieve the same momentum as a heavier lead weight that the exra speed is self-defeating. Speed compounds the ill effects of air resistance; control suffers. The faster the rod moves, the more difficult it becomes to time and execute the cast.

A conveniently generous chunk of lead works wonders for long range fishing. Momentum provides the answer: a six ounce sinker travelling at half the speed of three ounces still generates the same carrying power. Bonus points are more leisurely casting and fewer backlashes when you cast into the wind. Once in flight, the sinker is less affected by bait and wind drag. Soft baits stay on the hook.

Comparing heavy and light sinkers is rather like

Conditions	3 ounces	4 ounces	5 ounces	6 ounces	8 ounces
Still air, no baits	160 yds	175 yds	190 yds	185 yds	160 yds
Still air + bait	100 yds	120 yds	135 yds	142 yds	140 yds
Headwind + bait	80 yds	90 yds	105 yds	115 yds	125 yds

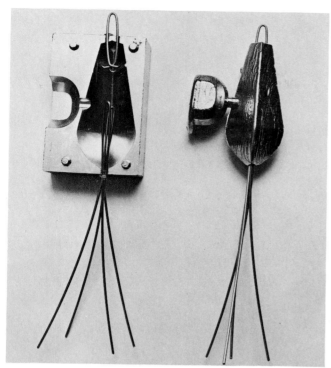

The DCA Aquapedo sinker rigged with fixed nosewires which are bent into grapnels for fishing in fast tides.

excellent compromise between easy casting and good carrying capacity. They are also best for learning to cast: start with 5 ounces and later experiment with sinkers weighing 5·25, 5·5, 5·75 and 6 ounces.

Quarter-ounce variations produce surprising results. Even without changing rod, reel or line, you will make your longest casts with one specific weight. For most anglers that will be 5·25 or 5·5 ounces, and the distances may be up to 20 yards better than with just ¼-ounce either side.

The same weight is also ideal for general fishing: it casts nicely with a full load of bait, anchors in all but the fastest tides, and penetrates an onshore breeze.

Smaller sinkers

Anglers who are dismayed by the loss of distance caused by exchanging a 5 ounce sinker for, say, 2 ounces usually fail to appreciate that the weight of projectile they cast—lure or sinker—must be balanced to line diameter and rod action. 2 ounces on 0·40 mm line is never much good for getting a big bait out there or for holding in the current.

2 ounces cast on 0·30 mm line (8–10 lb test) is another matter. Distances shoot up and the lower water resistance of the line encourages firm tackle anchorage. Provided bait is relatively small, you can fish at 125 yards. Lures produce much the same response, though low-density plugs never do fly as far as a streamlined bar of steel like the Hopkins lure.

measuring cars against trucks. For the same engine capacity, one goes faster, the other carries a bigger load. From the beach, this load capacity is the deciding factor. Additionally, a big sinker holds better in the tide and boosts tackle inertia, perhaps the most important aid to hooking fish at long range. A series of tests carried out over grass pinpoint the strengths and weaknesses of sinker weights. Figures in this table relate to casts made on standard pendulum tackle, 0·40 mm main line and a Penn 970 reel.

The conclusions are self-evident. As far as distance is concerned, choice of sinker weight diminishes in step with drag no matter how it is caused. In practical terms, long range beach fishing demands at least 5 ounces of lead with the standard pendulum rod, reel and line. 3 ounces is fine for short-range fishing in calm weather. 5–6 ounces are excellent for all-round fishing and actually cast a bait farther than 8 ounce sinkers. However, when the wind is blowing hard onshore, the sluggish big weight outclasses the rest. For all-round success in the surf you need a selection of sinkers to accommodate weather, tidal pull and distance.

The results of even limited tests show that 5–6 ounces of lead are close to perfect with ordinary beach tackle, baited or not. Tournament casters in Britain settle for 5·25 ounces or close to it. There is a definite link between 5–6 ounces and the casting ability and strength of the majority of fishermen. Sinkers in this weight band provide an

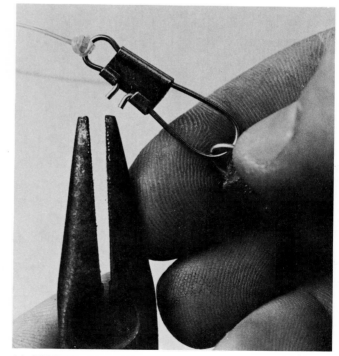

It's ESSENTIAL to buffer the sinker knot against abrasion on the seabed. Tough split rings and secure safety-pin links are safe enough for routine fishing. Guard against cheap clips that tear open under pressure.

Sinker weight/line test combinations for high-performance casting

$\frac{5}{8}$–1 ounce . . . 4–10 lb test (0·25–0·30 mm diameter)

1–3 ounce . . . 8–12 lb test (0·275–0·35 mm diameter)

Practical fishing distances in reasonably good weather should be around 125 yards with 1 ounce metal lures cast on 8 lb test. 2–3 ounces on 10 lb test will fly 150 yards—perhaps more in perfect conditions with Hopkins lures and others of sound aerodynamic design. Zoned action rods of the correct length and power are absolutely essential, as are small, high-peformance reels like the Penn Spinfisher 650SS and Levelmatic, ABU 5000 series baitcasters, Daiwa Magforce and Shakespeare Sigmas. Do not expect to hit the heights with ordinary surf reels—less than 2 ounces do not provide enough momentum in the cast to make the spool turn fast enough.

Sinker shapes

Only one shape of sinker makes sense for long-range fishing . . . nothing compares to a bomb or torpedo design with a round or square cross-section. Pyramids, bank sinkers, 'Grip' weights and the rest of the traditional and exotic shapes of sinkers are all inferior. It is a waste of time and effort to develop an excellent casting style, then destroy its benefits with an inefficient sinker.

Sinker shape affects the cast in three distinct areas—turn-over, flight and seabed control.

Turn over is the brief but important phase of the cast immediately before line release. The sinker starts by swinging nose down on the pendulum arc. As full power forces the blank into full compression and your arms take over to add the final punch and pull, it flips through 180 degrees to fly nose first into the sky. This turn-over, coming so close to full power and reel release, is inevitably accompanied by severe whiplashing. Inferior sinkers wobble and flirt through the air, lose energy and destroy baits by literally tearing them from the hook.

The phenomenon is much exaggerated with fixed spool reels, which have a much faster and more vicious line release than multipliers. Sometimes the wobble is so severe and prolonged that the rod tip oscillates violently—a frequent cause of trapped leader knots and line tangles. The inertia of a multiplier spool imposes a degree of control on the turning sinker but does not eliminate ragged flight.

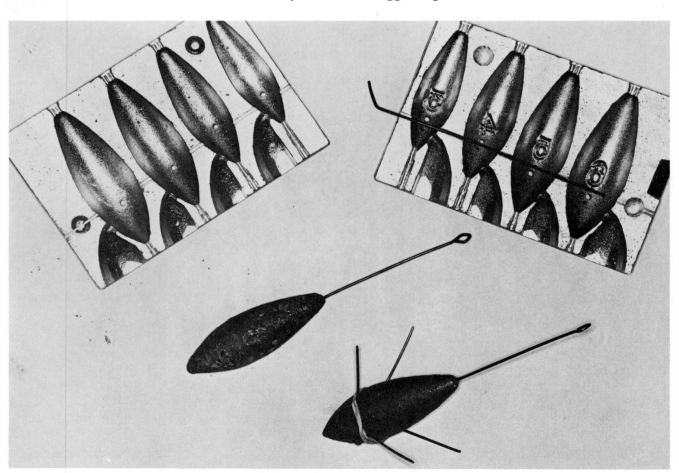

Certainly the best sinker on the beach—the DCA Beachcomb fitted with a long tail wire and optional swivelling grip wires.

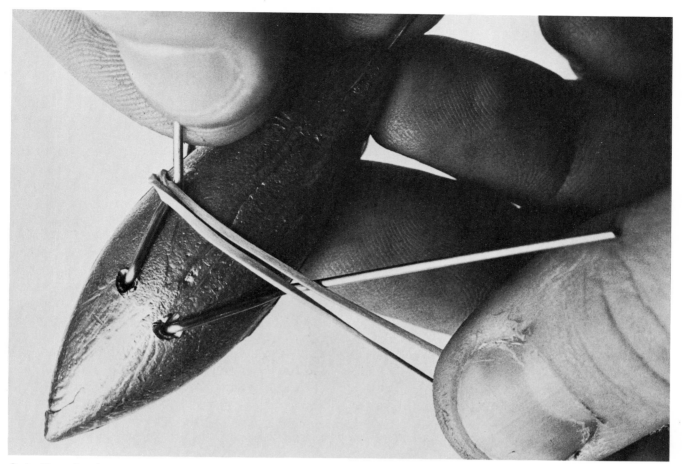

Swivelling grip-wires are more comfortable for fishing because they offer no resistance on retrieve. Make your own sinkers with rubber band security straps. Adjust the pressure so that the wires hold steady until triggered by striking.

In-flight stability helps the sinker cut neatly through the air. You want a 'dead', fully stabilised flight, not one that encourages the sinker to flip from side to side. The faster and lighter the sinker or lure, the more effect shape has on flight path. Cast extremely hard, a leaf-shaped hollow-section lure blade may actually boomerang back on itself to dive, turn 90 degrees left or right, or even take off vertically for the heavens. Heavier lead sinkers towing baits just lose energy, pick up the wind and drop short of the mark. A severe, prolonged wobble originating from the initial turn-over could easily destroy multiplier tuning and cause backlash. Many 'inexplicable' backlashes are directly the result of poor sinker design—check sinker shape if you are plagued by continual casting problems with no obvious solution. The best caster in the world could not control some of the sinkers widely available for surfcasting.

Seabed control. Is the acid test of any sinker efficient enough to get out there in the first place. Once on the seabed, the sinker must either anchor terminal rig and bait, or allow a steady, controlled drift downstream. All kinds of shapes and sizes of sinker were tested during the early days of long-

range British surfcasting. Only the grip-wired bomb has survived. 'Watch' leads, pyramids and the rest are totally inferior.

Serious though the design criteria of surf sinkers may appear, the answer is absolutely straightforward. Bombs turn over nicely, fly neatly through the sky, and, wired with swivelling or fixed spikes of stainless steel, hold bottom in the fiercest current. Look no further than the bomb concept for excellent surf fishing.

Short bombs, like the DCA Aquapedo with its characteristic square cross-section, are good all-rounders. The latest Beachbomb sinkers from the same manufacturer are even better in some respects—the lower air drag seems to add a couple of yards to the cast. The Aquazoom sinker, also from DCA Moulds (address: 41, Lon Isa, RHIWBINA, Cardiff CF4, 6EE, WALES) is now officially chosen for all British tournaments. No other company in the world has done more research and development on casting sinker shape. Their range of die-cast aluminium alloy moulds is absolutely unbeatable, and available in all sizes from 2 to 10 ounces, including the 5·25 (150 gramme) competition standard.

Adding the grip wires

Plain sinkers are fine for casting practice and still-water fishing. It may be better to drift along the seabed anyway, in which case you can control the rate by adding or subtracting lead. It is a neat way of pinpointing underwater gulleys—the sinker swings around with the tide and drops into the depression; the tide does not have enough force to roll it up the far side. Drumfish and cod anglers use this trick to position their baits to best advantage on beaches which do not dry out enough at low water to expose the foreshore structure.

On the whole, wired sinkers are more versatile. Mould four stainless wires, some 4–6 inches long, into a bomb's nose. Bend them into grapnels, and you will find that the sinker will hold fast in most tidal currents. 5 ounce wired sinkers hold better than 10 ounces of plain lead.

Fixed wires tend to catch in the seabed on retrieve. The Breakaway sinker, either shop-bought or made at home, features swivelling wires moulded close to the sinker's nose and held under tension by a rubber band, or beads trapped in sinker flank depressions by wire tension alone. The sinker casts and fishes extremely well and pulls ashore with minimal resistance. However, once in position, the sinker has to stay put. Moving it triggers the wires and destroys the grip.

For that reason a fixed-wire sinker is useful in conditions which demand that baits be kept on the move. Keen surf men keep both in their tackle boxes.

Long-tailed sinkers

Sinkers with extended tail wires instead of normal short loops have made a big impact on the British market since their introduction from Spain, where they were developed to boost the efficiency of fixed spool casting. Instead of moulding in a normal loop, insert 4–6 inches of stiff wire into the back of the mould. Bend the far end into a strong loop for leader clip attachment.

A long-tailed sinker almost completely stabilises the turn-over phase and proceeds, dart-like, into the sky. Even multiplier casts are smoothed; and smoothness automatically exploits the full power of the cast, resulting in a few extra yards. More important, you lose less distance on a bad cast as the sinker irons out small mistakes. The altered geometry of a grip-wired sinker fitted with a long tail boosts anchorage quite significantly. A 5 ounce long-tail holds in the current as securely as a 6 ounce conventionally-looped bomb. As the message spreads through surfcasting, this Spanish development is sure the become THE sinker preferred by casters all over the world.

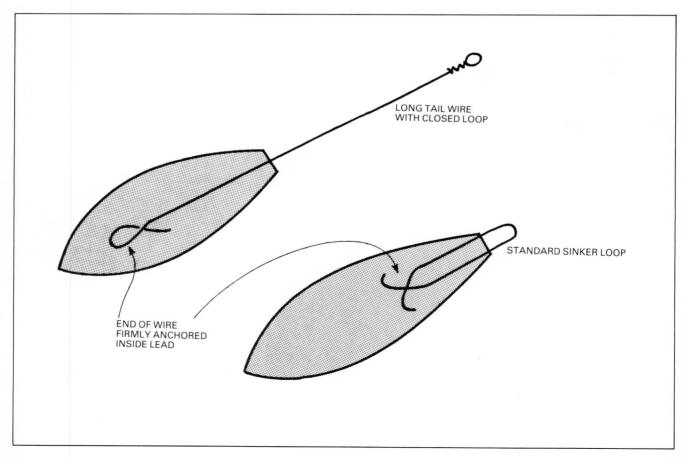

LONG TAIL WIRE
WITH CLOSED LOOP

STANDARD SINKER LOOP

END OF WIRE
FIRMLY ANCHORED
INSIDE LEAD

Terminal Rigs and the Baitsafe Capsule

When you have cut through all the technical and subjective aspects of fishing—sport, competition, relaxation, tackle development and whatever else holds your interest—the entire success of the sport will rely on a fish opening its mouth and swallowing the hook. Bait presentation is the deciding factor, and good bait presentation boils down to casting an attractive offering into the fish's path. Get that wrong, and you are beaten.

Rods, reels, lines and casting style apply equally to natural bait and artificial lure fishing; and to some extent it does not matter whether you fish in freshwater or salt. But at this point—bait presentation—we are looking specifically at natural baits.

Natural baits presented on, or, close to the seabed, stationary in the current or slowly drifting, impose special restrictions. Success is a mixture of dropping the tackle in the right general area, then making the fish swim up to it. Presentation, then, is a combination of casting perfomance and natural bait attraction by sight, taste and smell. The farther you cast, the more dificult it is for traditional tackle to maintain its efficiency. Beyond 125 yards, most old-time rigs simply do not catch fish. Bait rips off in mid-cast. Sinkers drift freely in the tide. Bite detection is impossible, and you cannot strike the hook home anyway. Good fishing results from presenting the right bait at the right time in the right place . . . and having the fish then hook itself. Many anglers spend most of their time on the beach fishing a bare hook: however often they do cast into the best spot, they still will not catch a thing.

The basic rigs—paternoster and running leger

Short traces with the sinker on the bottom cast very well and certainly hook a lot of fish. Choose one, two or three hooks according to species, distance and conditions. For routine fishing in European waters, and especially for bottom-feeding small fishes like flounders, dabs, soles, whiting and eels, a double or triple hooked paternoster is excellent. Cheap to make, simple to fish and adequately sophisticated to hook those species which feed by smell and are not fussy anyway, it is the unviersal terminal tackle for beginners and experts alike.

I tie a bunch of paternosters at home and bundle them, without snoods and hooks, into a plastic bag. On the beach I attach the paternoster to the end of the leader, then arrange hooks according to conditions and the baits that I am about to fish.

The central rib of a paternoster always begins at the upper end with a strong ring or swivel (Mustad, Berkley or Dexter) and ends with a split ring for sinker attachment. Length of the centre rib varies according to number of hooks and expected species. On average, you cannot go far wrong with two or three snoods (a snood is the piece of nylon linking hook to paternoster) spaced 18 inches apart with 18 inches between lower loop and sinker clip, and at least 6 inches gap between upper loop and leader joint.

The central rib is an extension of the leader as well as part of the terminal rig. You cannot expect the sinker to remain safely attached unless the breaking strain of the rib is at least as high as the main leader. An extra 10 per cent breaking strain compensates for the many knots in the trace. Tie Palomar or Uni-knots top and bottom. Ordinary stand-off loops, plain or twisted for stiffness, withstand even long distance casting pressures; however, if you are worried about snap-offs, try using a swivel trapped between two Superglued stoppers for each snood. Extra stiffness and reduction of snood twist are provided by a short piece of plastic tube slid over each loop.

Variations on the two-hook paternoster theme are triple-hook rigs for competition fishing and single-hook, heavy duty rigs for cod and channel bass. Space loops accordingly; adjust the length of the central rib as necessary.

Snood lengths are seldom critical. Short snoods cast more cleanly, help retain baits on the hook and are less likely to tangle. They also jerk the fish up short and make it hook itself. On the other hand, longer snoods encourage some species to bite more freely. Bigger fish, cod especially, need a snood long enough to be sucked deeply into their throats for a firm hookhold. Breaking strain of the snood ought to be the lightest compatible with the expected species. Extra diameter/abrasion resistance is useful for warding off sharp teeth and scaly fins.

Two Hook Paternoster

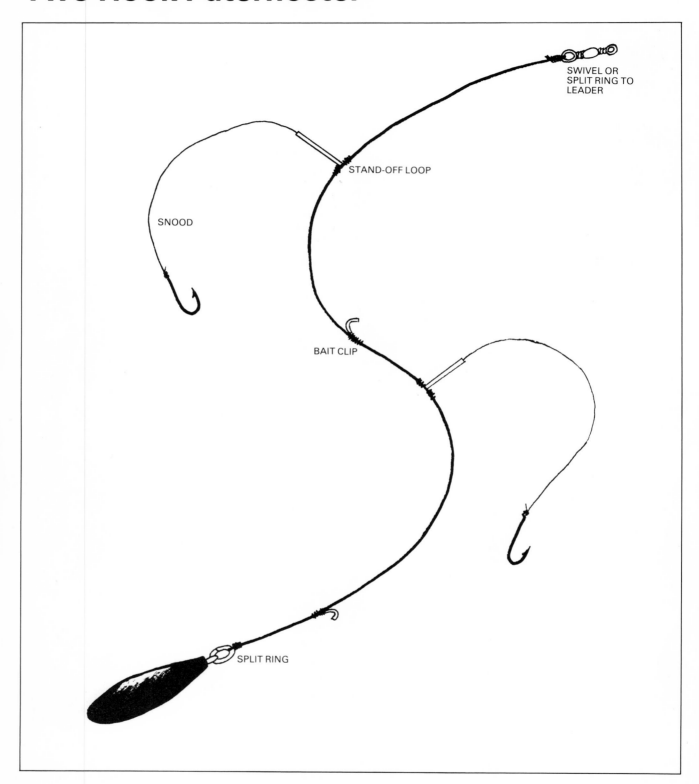

SWIVEL OR
SPLIT RING TO
LEADER

STAND-OFF LOOP

SNOOD

BAIT CLIP

SPLIT RING

PATERNOSTER GUIDE

Species	Overall length	No. of hooks	Snood length	Snood test
COD	48 in.	1–2	9–18 in.	15–30 lb.
FLATFISH	36–60 in.	2–3	6–12 in.	10–15 lb.
WHITING	36–60 in.	2–3	6–9 in.	15–25 lb.
BASS	36–48 in.	1–2	12–18 in.	12–20 lb.

Single-hook paternoster for heavyweight species

Big cod, channel bass and stripers, tope and conger eels can easily ruin a standard paternoster; and of course, you need only one hook on the rig. Modify the ordinary paternoster this way: Shorten the central rib to 24 inches of 40–50 lb test monofilament. Attach upper swivel and lower split ring as before, and tie in a big stand-off loop about 12 inches above the sinker. The snood is 12–24 inches of 25–50 lb monofil (80 lb monofil or 50 lb cable-laid wire for conger) tied or crimped to the loop, which is stiffened with 3 inches of thick-wall plastic tube. Although longer than the loop to sinker dimension, the snood still fishes without tangles.

As an alternative, make a running paternoster (also useful for the smaller species as well if the materials are scaled down). Slide a small, strong swivel directly onto the leader and follow it with a small nylon bead. Then tie the usual swivel or a split ring to the end of the leader. Connect the hook to the split ring with the same 24 inch trace. This time, though, tie in another 24 inch piece of leader-test nylon between the running swivel and the sinker, which must also be connected by split ring, and never directly tied to the nylon. The bait hangs next to the sinker for casting, flies quite well, and creates less tackle resistance when a fish picks up the bait and runs with it.

The standard running leger

For short range fishing in calm or slow moving water, traditional legers may be successful with shy-biting species. Overall, however, they offer no clear advantages and few long-distance casters bother to use them for everyday work. The over-long trace does not pick up cleanly from the pendulum swing, whiplashes bait off the hook, and helicopters the hook around the leader. When clean casts and long distances are essential for good sport, the running leger is just a damn nuisance.

Bait clips—the key to better distances

Bait whiplash on release and in-flight air drag are markedly reduced by restraining hooks and snoods close to the leader. You can add up to 30 yards to maximum fishing distance by clipping down all three snoods of a match-fishing paternoster rather than leaving them to flap in the air currents. Gains are just as significant with a single cod, bass or drumfish rig baited with whole squid, mullet, mackerel or kingsize bunch of worms.

Cut half the bend from a fine-wire long-shanked hook about 5 mm in gape. Slide the leader through the hook eye—it does not matter if you position the hook above or below the stand-off

The bait clip ready to cast. The cut-off hook traps the baited trace against the leader until the sinker hits the water.

A Leger Stop (available from freshwater tackle shops) or a nylon stop-knot prevent bait sliding too far up the trace.

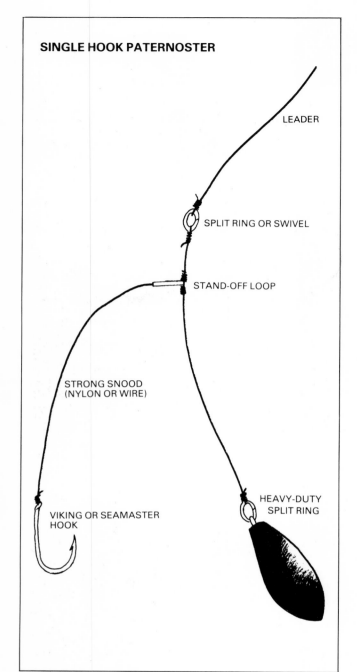

SINGLE HOOK PATERNOSTER

LEADER

SPLIT RING OR SWIVEL

STAND-OFF LOOP

STRONG SNOOD
(NYLON OR WIRE)

HEAVY-DUTY
SPLIT RING

VIKING OR SEAMASTER
HOOK

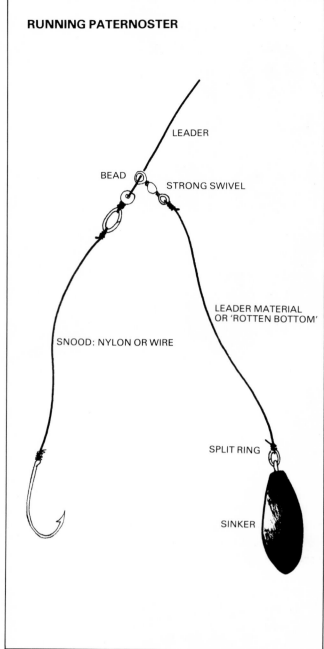

RUNNING PATERNOSTER

LEADER

BEAD

STRONG SWIVEL

LEADER MATERIAL
OR 'ROTTEN BOTTOM'

SNOOD: NYLON OR WIRE

SPLIT RING

SINKER

loop—and whip the shank to the leader with 6 lb test monofilament. Make the whipping fairly tight, so that the hook slides under pressure but does not move at the slightest excuse. Now arrange the cut-off hook so that its bend, and that of the baited hook, loosely but securely interlock. The cut-off hook retains the baited hook throughout the cast, but releases it as soon as the leader slackens, which it invariably does on hitting the sea. The idea is neat and simple and the only important point is to get the tension right initially. Move the cut-off bait clip up or down the leader until its position is exactly right for security in flight and immediate release at the other end. It is a trial and error job.

Small 'L' shaped pieces of brass wire sleeved to the leader with half an inch of plastic tube are equally effective as bait clips. Leger Stops with a bent wire insert work nicely as well. As long as the clip is correctly positioned and fairly open in the bend, it can be made up from all kinds of wires, sleeves, hooks and whippings. Thicker wires seem to provide better release than narrow guage materials.

Some anglers clip the snoods up the trace, others favour an under-loop clip. Small baits on multi-hook paternosters work well either way, but there is some advantage in clipping a single, bulky bait as close as possible behind the sinker. Bait rides in the slipstream.

THE BAITSAFE CAPSULE

Suffolk anglers Ted Thwaites and Alan Morrell manufacture and market what probably amounts to the most significant development in surf casting—and freshwater natural bait fishing—this decade. Their Baitsafe casting capsule is a space-age answer to the eternal headaches of bait loss and air drag. In its way, this space shuttle of the surfline takes long-distance surf casting one step nearer perfection. It also holds the key to better fishing for anglers who do not have to cast far or cannot be bothered to learn.

The Baitsafe capsule, available in nominal 4, 5 and 6 ounce models, is a tough, injection moulded plastic box with one open side covered in flight by a hinged door. Cynics reckon it looks like a flying coffin. The front of the box contains the casting weight—a specially shaped chunk of lead permanently bonded to the plastic and immune to casting pressure. The lead is drilled for two pairs of optional grip wires which operate in exactly the same way as the spikes of a bomb sinker.

The back of the plastic shell is hollow. Rig the trace above the Baitsafe, bait the hook, tuck it inside the box and clip on the lid. Bait and sinker are now packaged for hard casting. The shape of the Baitsafe, though rather unsophisticated in appearance, is aerodynamically sound—the cast flies cleanly and far distant.

A special rubber pad cushions the lid in flight. It stays on no matter how hard or far you cast. Immediately on hitting the sea, the lid flies off and releases the bait from the box. Release is triggered by the force of the Baitsafe's impact with water—a pressure of over 20 lb a square inch, more than enough to override the clip mechanism.

A Baitsafe on the seabed grips just as strongly as a sinker of the same weight. In fact it seems to hold even better than a fixed-wire lead. And as soon as you start to retrieve, the capsule takes off like a rocket for the surface. Within 20 yards of leaving the seabed, it is on top and surfing back across the waves. You can imagine how useful that is over rough ground which traps conventional tackle.

All right, so the Baitsafe casts well, holds bottom and stands more chance of surviving rough ground. What else can it do? The totally enclosed bait compartment holds a fair sized bait. Reduced drag adds yards to the cast—at least equalling the results of bait clips. And that is just the beginning.

Any bait inserted into the capsule is totally immune to whiplash and air pressure. You can cast the softest baits imaginable, confident that when the lid flies off out to sea you are fishing a

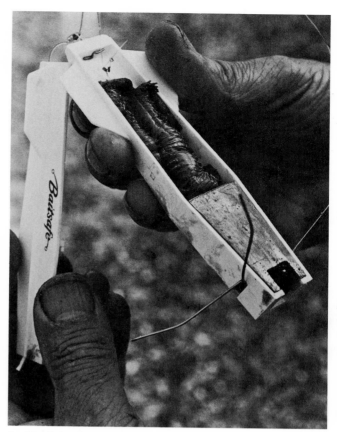

1 *The Baitsafe capsule opened for loading. Tuck baited hook and trace inside the plastic case which holds the lead weight as well.*

2 *Clip on the flat cover, then cast the Baitsafe as a streamlined package which protects the bait from air damage and whiplash.*

perfectly presented bait. Jelly-soft crabs, watery mussel, harbour ragworms or cream cheese for mullet. The Baitsafe excels with them all.

The idea of packaging baits for long distance work has intrigued surf and freshwater anglers for decades. Only now with Ted and Alan's device on the market are anglers free to experiment with soft baits, super-light traces and small hooks, semi-buoyant rigs and groundbaiting (chumming) at long range.

Send an S.A.E. to Intakl Angling, P.O. Box 8, BECCLES, Suffolk, for full details. The device is sold through tackle shops and direct. Do not imagine for one moment that here is one more gimmick to waste a surfman's money. The Baitsafe is a work of importance and sheer genius, a landmark in fishing tackle design.

Hooks for surfcasting

Size of hooks, their design and performance create all kinds of problems for anglers who fish surf and freshwater. Massive hooks, robust wire and specially shaped points and bends are traditionally used for saltwater fishing. Freshwater anglers adopt a more flexible approach and to my mind they teach saltwater anglers some hard lessons. We would catch more fish from surf, estuaries and rockmarks by reducing hook size, of that I am sure.

It may well be forced upon us to investigate better terminal rigs in general and hooks in particular. Falling fish stocks and greater competition between anglers have the same long-term effect in the surf as became clear in freshwater fishing some twenty years ago – fine tackle catches more fish.

The strength of the bigger traditional fishing hooks is largely wasted. What is the value of a 2 ton breaking strain hook on a line that pops at 12 pounds? None at all, save for some protection against the fish's teeth and jaws. And of course a hook must be big enough to accommodate a large bait when necessary. Sheer gape, shank length and point durability ensure we do not reduce the wire diameter and steel temper below reasonable levels. However, there is still plenty of leeway for experiment.

For some years I have progressively reduced the size of my hooks—in wire diameter, barb height and bend. Only shank length remains static— fairly long to assist self-striking by the fish. The lighter I go, the more bites I get. It is true that smaller hooks encourage smaller fish, but you can always throw them back. Small hooks DEFINITELY DO NOT lose your big fish or even deter their biting in the first place. You will almost certainly find yourself catching and landing more

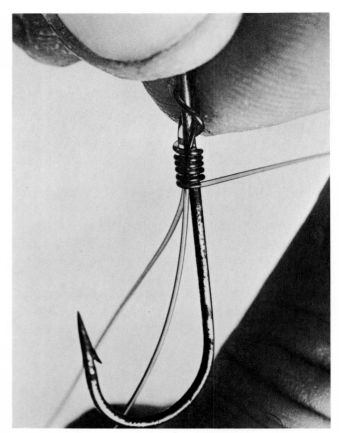

Surface rust and corrosion are almost inevitable. Deeper damage than this should be rejected. This is a medium-guage wire Aberdeen hook for cod fishing.

Small, well tempered hooks are more than a match for heavy fish hooked in the surf.

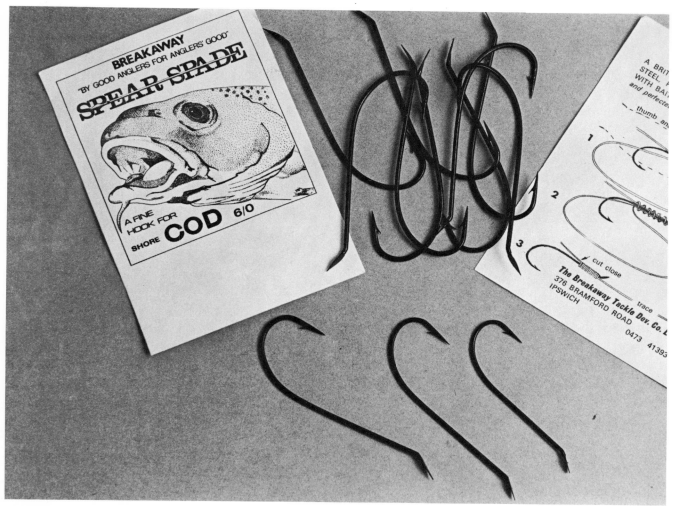

Spearpoint hooks—typical of modern high-performance surf hooks which ensure easy penetration at long range. The high-carbon steel hook is tough and razor sharp.

fish then ever. And you will miss far fewer bites.

For British and European sport, fine wire Aberdeen-type hooks between sizes 4 and 8/0 are the foundation of successful legering with natural baits cast long, medium or short range. Blue-steel Mustad are the sharpest of all; Partridge are tougher. The Breakaway Spearpoint and Spear-spade hooks, though not strictly Aberdeen-shaped, are a viable alternative, being extremely tough and sharp, well tempered and small-eyed.

More substantial hooks for big cod and bass, conger and tope range from the Mustad Vikings through to the smaller sizes of Seamaster game hooks. Again, it pays to reduce the hook size to the practical minimum compatible with bait size. Here the Baitsafe helps prevent baits tearing from a small hook. Cast unprotected, a bait should be thoroughly skewered by bend and shank.

Small hooks can be rigged to accept big baits.

The lower inches of the snood or trace replace the missing bend and shank as bait support. You simply thread the baits around the bend, up the shank, over the eye and on to the monofilament. The trouble is that they keep right on sliding and at the end of the cast they are tight against the paternoster stand-off loop.

Prevent this by tying a separate stop-knot on to the snood just above the hook eye. Make it of stiffish nylon—around 12 lb test—and leave the ends protruding by ½ inch so they prevent baits sliding too far. When the knot is suitably positioned, you can cram plenty of bait on to a small hook. As long as the bend and point are exposed, the hook will trap a biting fish just as easily as a larger bend would. Being thinner in the wire, a small hook gets a firm grip and sinks below the barb with no need for heavy striking or high line tension.

Back-casting

Back casting, also called Yarmouth or Norfolk-style, cannot be confused with any other casting technique. Instead of standing head-on to the water and casting with a final punch-pull of the arms, you face away from the water and 'shovel' the rod over your shoulder. It is a rough and ready way to cast, specialised in application but nevertheless too important to ignore. Some fishing cries out for the back-cast.

Though there are seldom occasions when the back-cast is the *only* way to fish, it is still a major force to be reckoned with. Distances are excellent, but the real strength of the back-cast is its easy, slow power stroke which handles very big sinkers when necessary. Soft baits are less likely to burst.

The back-cast technique

First a word of warning. The back-cast is dangerous. Performed well, on an open beach and with a strong shock leader matched to a good rod and reel, the cast is no worse than any other. Unfortunately, it is a style which lends itself to brute power, and the result, inevitably, is that anglers with little or no experience stand in the middle of a crowd and lash into their interpretation of the style. The danger is that the sinker might fly off along the beach rather than out to sea. The message is plain to anyone with an ounce of commonsense: practise on a deserted beach, and keep the power down until you master the swing and pull-through. Then the cast is as safe as any other, although it does demand more space than the normal pendulum. Good back-casters are perfectly safe because they appreciate the limitations of the style, which is totally inappropriate from piers and jetties, on crowded beaches and from rocks.

The back-cast is an extension of the old-time handline fishing style used along the East Coast of England. Nineteenth-century fishermen (and a few of today's traditionalists) learned to increase the range of their handline tackle by levering the coiled line seawards on a casting pole—a six foot stick with a spike on top used to boost the normal arc of throwing. Substitute rod and reel for handline and pole, and you have the elements of the modern back-cast.

Back-casters take up position with their backs to the sea. The sinker hangs on a massive leader drop which is often longer than the normal 13–14·5 foot rod necessary for this technique. A right

1 *Stand back to the sea. Tuck the reel into your right hip and extend your left arm well up the handle. Swing the sinker on a long drop—push it towards, just as in normal pendulum casting . . .*

4 *Guide the rod—still at full power—into an upward arc. Get your full body weight behind the handle. Use your legs too.*

2 ... then pull the tackle back so that the sinker swings behind your shoulder. When you feel the sinker pause at the top of the arc ...

3 ... sweep the handle around and down, building power as quickly as possible.

5 Release at the peak of the lifting action. The sinker flies extremely high with this style. Direction control may be difficult at first.

6 Hold the rod tip high until the sinker and tackle splash into the water.

handed caster would hold the top handle grip of the rod in his left hand. The right hand cradles rod butt cap and low-set reel hard against the right hip bone.

The casts begins with a pendulum swing similar to that of the normal pendulum style and the left hand pushes the sinker away to the limit of body rotation—just as in the pendulum cast. The body guides the long rod to sweep the pendulum in-swing high above and to the rear of the caster's head. Then the main power stroke is a smooth, fast body and left hand sweep which levers the rod around and upwards to release point. Similarity to pitchforking a bale of hay backwards over your shoulder is probably no coincidence—the original handline back-casters were farm labourers well versed in haymaking and harvesting. It is a natural body action, easy to develop and always powerful due to the free application of body weight. Most people can pull harder than they can push.

Tackle for the back-cast

The back-cast is relatively slow and lacks the final arm and shoulder acceleration of standard casting techniques. On the other hand it is extremely powerful, so you can compensate for lack of butt speed by increasing tip length. 13 feet is regarded as short for a back-caster; more experienced anglers prefer at least 13·5 feet for fishing and may go as high as 15 feet for tournament casting. Length of rod is no deterrent to casting, but is a high price to pay in general fishing—heavy, imbalanced, and hard work with a big fish on the end.

The length and weight of the blank make it a non-starter for anglers who fish in surf where the rod cannot be rested. Lure fishing is almost certainly too strenuous with a back-cast rod. The style originated on cod and whiting beaches where you cast out and then wait for fish to detect your bait, so it is not surprising to find that even with modern rods and reels the back-cast has not spread to shore angling in general. The vast majority of back-casters live in Suffolk and Norfolk, or farther up the coast—Newcastle and Hull—where the traditional styles of fishing were also founded on handline and pole.

Critics of back-casting attack its crudeness; from the truly sporting point of view they are probably right. The rod is a monster—8·5 feet of powerful glassfibre joined to maybe 6 feet of 1·25 inch diameter aluminium alloy butt do not really inspire the majority of saltwater anglers. But they cannot disregard its effectiveness and sheer power.

Very few back-casters bother with a multiplier reel, however there is no reason why you should not use one—except that you will find spool grip and cast control a little more difficult than it is on a normal pendulum outfit. Fixed spool is preferred because it is so much easier to handle—no trouble with spool release, no backlashes of course, and much better balance and power in retrieve. Tucked low down beside your right hip, the reel lies in a most comfortable and natural position. Grip the upper handle with an almost straight arm and then just lean back on the rod to apply full pressure to terminal rig and hooked fish.

Terminal rig, traces and lines are identical to those used in normal casting. You will find it easier to handle big sinkers—6, 7 and 8 ounces are perfectly feasible. (They are just as easy on ordinary pendulum tackle but you do need a far higher level of expertise to avoid burned thumbs and strained rod). In fact, back-casters tend to standardise on heavier than normal terminal rigs which may well prove more effective on East Coast cod grounds.

Advantages of the back-cast

Powerful casting with a slow, relaxed body sweep and no particular emphasis on arm acceleration comes into its own in winter. Thick clothing and frozen fingers are more restrictive in multiplier reel casting with a short pendulum rod than in fixed spool back-casting. Although you may well be able to cast farther in ideal weather with your forward-facing style, the back-cast is a valuable alternative for fishing in conditions which might otherwise persuade you to go home. You may even grow to like it for its own sake as well.

Mostly, however, it is the way to handle big seas, rough weather and low temperatures. Dedicated back-casters may well argue that their style is far more versatile, but the tiny numbers of anglers who fish that way prove that this is not by any means a popular or even interesting way to approach general beach fishing. Like many anglers, I use it as a specific weapon for isolated circumstances; I cannot imagine why anyone would want to use it all the time, unless they fish the same old beaches for the same old species year after year. Nobody could argue that back-casting fails to produce the goods, but there is more to fishing than sheer mechanics. In particular, who would want to lug around such a diabolical chunk of fishing rod for bassing, rock fishing and other situations where a shorter, lighter rod offers better handling and more enjoyable fishing? Angling is a pastime, not a survival exercise.

However, when those big waves drive in on the cod beaches, and wind whips spray and sand straight into your face, back-casting 7 or 8 ounces of lead out there far enough to drop a bunch of worms into a gulley where the fish run is a tremendous advantage, which, in my view, more than justifies building a back-cast rod and learning to use it. Maybe you fish that way ten days a year, but those may be times that cod fishing is at its peak. If ordinary tackle will not toss a bait far enough or will not anchor in the tide long enough to attract a fish, you might lose the opportunity to land a 20 pounder. These days cod have the habit of not coming back to give you a second shot. They are more choosy about moving inshore than ever they were, and if they do show up in big numbers, you can bet the weather and seas will be rough and cold. The best fishing often coincides with storms blowing straight in from the open sea and temperatures below zero.

Night fishing is ten time better . . . but further aggravates ordinary pendulum casting with free-running reel. Sometimes it is impossible to fish that way. Big, slow-flying sinkers are much kinder to soft baits. You will find night fishing with a heavy back-cast outfit brings a greater confidence:

you know within reason that baits hit the seabed rather than explode from the hook in mid-cast. During the day, whichever style you cast, you will see the baits travel all the way or shower into the breakers. If necessary, wind in, rebait and cast again. At night you have to take a chance that all went well—and that is where a back-caster and 7 ounces of lead pay off: when you are striving for maximum range with half a dozen soft lugworms aimed at those big cod. Plenty of night fishermen miss big catches because they fish without baits three casts out of four.

The extra carrying capacity of a big sinker may be useful for matchfishing with the three permitted hooks, each baited differently with a substantial hookload. Back-casters manage very well here. 7 or 8 ounces of lead will carry a peeler crab, two lugworms and, on the third hook, a four inch piece of king ragworm. Distances could be 25 yards more than with a 5 ounce ordinary pendulum outfit which would tend to mash baits, anyway. In addition, extremely long back-cast sinker drops accommodate three snoods over 7 or 8 feet of leader, whereas on a shorter rod you would need to compress the paternoster loops into 6 feet at most.

Index

A

Aberdeen hook, 91
ABU, 58
Action, 45
Air drag, 9
Aluminium alloy, 44

B

Backlash, 60
Bait clip, 87
Baitsafe, 89
Blank
    carbon fibre, 42
    'E' glassfibre, 41
    'S' glassfibre, 41
Boron, 45
Brakes
    centrifugal, 62
    magnetic, 63
Bruce & Walker, 41
Butt
    construction, 44
    pressure test, 33

C

Cast
    back cast, 92
    level line, 74
    overhead, 13
    South African, 19
Confidence, 11
Corrosion, 57

D

DAM 5001, 65
Diameter
    blank, 36
    butt, 44
    line, 79
    tip, 33
Drop, 16, 24

E

Effective length, 40
Effort, 9

F

Fenwick, 34
Feralite, 44
Finger guard, 73
Fittings, 53–54
Friction 8, 52

G

Grips, 53
Grip wires, 84

H

Handle length, 53
Head position, 18
Hooks, 91
Hybrid ring pattern, 49

I

Inner tube, 54
Inswing, 26

J

Javelin action, 18

K

Knot
    Bimini twist, 75
    leader, 75
    timber hitch, 59
    Uni knot, 85

L

Layout, 16, 18
Level wind, 59
Loop
    Stand-off, 85
    Stiffener, 87

M

Modification
    coning, 70
    drag lock, 73
    level wind, 59
    profiling, 67

N

Night fishing, 95

O

Obstructions, 64
Off-ground cast, 18–19
Oil, 63
Outswing, 26

P

Paternosters, 85–87
Penn reels
    Levelmatic, 57
    Magpower 970, 58
    Spinfisher, 65, 71
    Squidder, 58
Punch-pull action, 16, 18

R

Reels
    capacity, 57, 59, 66, 70
    drag system, 57, 67
    lubrication, 63
    models, 57–59
    sidecaster, 73
Rings, 48–52
Rods
    action, 41
    length, 33, 43
    materials, 41–44

S

Semi-carbon, 43
Shock leader
    breaking strain, 75
    knots, 75
    length, 76
Sinker
    DCA Aquapedo, 81
    DCA Beachbomb, 82
    moulds, 83
    shape, 80
    weight, 81, 82
Snoods, 85
Spearpoint hook, 91
Split rings, 85

T

Tapers, 35, 47
Tidal currents, 80
Tournaments, 5
Traces, 85–87

W

Weight transfer, 19
Whiplash, 82
Winter fishing, 94
Working the rod, 13